3 NO-FAIL LIFE HABITS

The 3 G Method to Rewire and Transform Your Brain, Body and Spirit

By Linda Larson Schlitz

Published by Purpose Driven Recovery Academy Publishing.

ISBN: 979-8-9964344-0-4

Privacy Notice

The stories in this book are based on real experiences and transformations. To protect client confidentiality, some names, identifying details, and circumstances have been changed. Other stories are shared with the permission of those involved. In all cases, these accounts are presented with respect and gratitude for the courage required to pursue sobriety and spiritual renewal.

ENDORSEMENTS

"Linda is someone who gets it. Over the past 18 years I've watched her gather real-world and academic experience, morphing into a first-rate counselor, speaker, and author.

The 3G's are bedrock principles of authentic substance abuse recovery, but Linda explores just how deep the rabbit hole goes, how these simple principles can literally rewire the way we think and process all life experience.

Her passion and ability to weave both clinical and spiritual threads, makes this a must read for anyone looking to break through to greater awareness and fulfillment in life."

David Brisbin
Pastor, Counselor, Author,
Founder of TheEffect Church/Recovery Community

"As a therapist and a person in long-term recovery, I found myself in early recovery wishing I had something like the 3G's. The simple practice of focusing on Gratitude, recognizing what I am Good At, and setting meaningful Goals could have helped me navigate many of the challenges, fears, and self-doubts that often accompanied me during early recovery and as I moved through life's transitions.

Linda's sense of humor and vulnerability helped me realize that I can heal, be vulnerable, and grow. Most importantly, never give up. As many will know, this saying is "Embrace The Suck"... but ya don't have to do it alone, and this book is a must-have."

Dr. David MacIntyre, PsyD, LPC
Director of Training & Development,
The Centre for Well-Being, Inc. Brainspotting Consultant

"Linda's book 3 No Fail Life Habits- The 3 G Method to Rewire and Transform Your Brain, Body and Spirit shares an easy way to improve mental health. As a mental health coach, I read this book and started implementing with clients immediately. I believe it should be something that everyone practices. Overall, the book is easy to read, informative, rooted in science, and offers Linda's years of experience in working with clients to improve mental health conditions. It's well written, funny, and compelling. The habits recommended are simple, to the point, and easy to remember.

Even my most neurodivergent high-achievers have benefited from this exercise. I recommend that every mental health practitioner read this book, learn the why behind each point and offer their patients these ideas."

Stephanie Kunkel MA
Best Selling Author, Corporate Trainer
and Owner of Perspective Shifters LLC

"If you are looking for a practice that will change your perspective and your life, look no further than this book by Linda Larson Schlitz. I first discovered the power of the 3 G's years ago in treatment, and after sharing the concept with Linda, I watched her transform it into a way of life for thousands of others. Through sharing it with all of her clients, the residents at our sober houses and her Facebook online community, she has shown how just a few minutes a day can shift your mindset and build a life of purpose.

They say I'm prejudiced because she's my wife, but the truth is, I've been a student of Linda's wisdom for years. She has a unique ability to see the future of personal growth and translate it into simple, daily habits. I am truly blessed to be by her side, and I know you will feel just as grateful for the guidance she offers in these pages."

Ralph Schlitz Jr.
Retired Co-Founder and Director of
Randlin Adult Family Care Homes Inc.

"3 No Fail Life Habits - The 3 G Method to Rewire and Transform Your Brain, Body and Spirit" is a complete road map for making a meaningful, mindful, and spiritual shift in life. Linda Larson-Schlitz candidly and light-heartedly writes a narrative for easing life's burdens in very practical and proactive ways!"

Rebecca Kermitz
Retired Owner/Manager of Low Income Rental Housing

"I listen to Sister Linda's message every week on Facebook and I have been a part of her 3 G's group for these last 3 years. Ralph reads from her last book every day and this new book about the 3 G's will be a real blessing. It has helped me very much. Sister Linda and Brother Ralph help us and our orphanage in Pakistan every month and they truly are living the way Jesus says. We are very grateful and blessed."

Evangelist Saul Gill
Pastor, Pakistan

"My name is Pastor Sam Daniel from India. For the past 27 years, I have been serving God's Ministry in the poor slums of India sharing God's love with them. God introduced me to Sister Linda during the COVID-19 pandemic; since then, she has provided immense financial support for both my ministry, my family and my son's Bible college

God has given her to me as a beloved sister. She is a servant of God who has prayed for me and greatly strengthened me whenever I shared my struggles with her. She is a mighty woman of God who teaches the Word every Saturday on the 'Rapha Blessing Ministry' page.

I believe that the 3 No Fail Life Habits is a wonderful book, authored by the Holy Spirit through Sister Linda, and will bring deliverance, healing, courage, and faith to many, proving to be a great blessing."

Yours,
Bonigala Sam Daniel
Pastor, Rapha Blessing Ministries, India.

"I spent decades learning what it means to truly be grateful, to accept that I am enough, and to set goals that align with my God-given purpose. I'm sharing these hard-won lessons now so you don't have to walk the long path I did. This book is the guide I wish I'd had when I first started my journey toward sobriety and peace."

TJ Feldman
Software Engineer Program Student,
Independent Contract Driver

"My journey to sobriety began in 1989, but the path was far from a straight line. After years of struggle, culminating in homelessness and a life-saving, six-bypass open-heart surgery, I felt like I had hit a dead end.

When Linda and Ralph took me in, they reminded me of things I had learned in treatment years earlier by getting me back on track with the simple, daily practice of the 3 G's.

Through the ongoing challenges of recovery and the physical pain following my surgeries, these tools became my anchor. They changed my life in ways I never thought possible. Today, I am clean, sober since 2014, and serving others as a head driver at an assisted living facility.

If you are looking for a way to transform your own path, I cannot recommend this book enough. The 3 G's work, and they will put you on the good path you've been searching for."

Christopher Baumann
Veteran, Head Driver at Rennes Assisted Living Facility

"The genius of Linda Larson Schlitz is that she is not trying to convince us of some new trend or novelty; she is pointing to an ancient way. With her help, we find joy in the journey, even when we stumble.

If we have any doubts about this ancient way (cleverly packaged as The 3 G's), she persuades us with scientific data and heart-warming testimonies.

Linda will help you open doors to joy, hope, and peace that you knew must exist somewhere; she has found these doors and is eager to guide you to them."

Aaron Winowiski,
Pastor, New Day Christian Church, Weston, WI

ACKNOWLEDGMENTS

First and foremost, I want to thank God for giving me life, liberty and the pursuit of happiness, which is why this book is coming to you. I have the freedom to share what He has done for me.

Then I want to thank Him for giving me my husband Ralph and the relationship we have that is centered on the great wisdom of the Bible and our relationship with our Heavenly Father. Ralph brought the idea for this book back from the treatment center he went to in 2008 and has continually inspired me by posting every day in both our Facebook @speaktomegodimlistening group and also posts the meditation reading from my book "Speak to Me God I'm Listening-365 Daily Meditations for Those Who Want to Hear God Answer Life's Toughest Questions on his personal page to inspire others. He has pushed me to finish this book and lovingly helped me fine tune it.

I am also grateful for Stephanie Kunkel who was not only a great business coach to get me rolling on this book in her writing challenge group, but also did the first overview of the book and moved things around so it made some semblance of order. She encouraged me and helped me set goals to get it done. This goes to show you that even though she is my niece and younger than my daughter, age doesn't matter. Being willing to use the gifts God has given you does.

I want to thank Tammy Obermeier who has been a good friend, colleague and fellow recovering person who has supported and encouraged me and countless others for the last 15 years. She not only did many great edits on the book but she also wrote the foreword.

I also want to thank all of the people who read this book and wrote awesome endorsements, including Pastor Aaron Winowiski, Pastor Dave Brisbin, Dr. David McIntyre, Ralph Schlitz, Rebecca Kermitz, Tammy Obermeier, Stephanie Kunkel, Pastor Bonigala Sam Daniel,

Evangelist Saul Gill, Chris Baumann and TJ Feldmann. I also really appreciate Joshua Swatosh, my blind friend, who listened to the whole book, found corrections that needed to be made and offered the feedback of it being “a fabulous book.”

FOREWORD

When I was asked to write the foreword for this book, I was both honored and humbled. Having had the privilege of editing this manuscript, it gave me the opportunity to reflect not only on the message you'll find in these pages, but also on the remarkable woman who wrote them and the unexpected way our paths first crossed.

I met Linda 15 years ago when I walked into our local Job Center looking for employment. At that time, she was working as a Career Counselor, but it didn't take long for our conversation to move beyond resumes and job applications. She quickly recognized my passion for serving people experiencing homelessness and those struggling with addiction and recovery.

She invited me to volunteer at the non-profit organization she and her husband had co-founded and managed. Randlin Adult Family Care Homes Inc was a recovery home that provided hope, stability, and a fresh start for men and women who were experiencing both homelessness and addiction.

Looking back, I realize that invitation changed far more than my schedule-it helped shape the direction of my own life and ministry in recovery. I served on the Board of Directors and eventually became the House Manager. I spent the next 7 years following in Linda's footsteps.

I may have first met the author through our shared passion for helping people find hope and healing, but as our conversations unfolded, I discovered much more about Linda. Her deep compassion, her remarkable professional expertise, and her unwavering commitment to helping others overcome trauma, addiction, and life's many challenges was evident.

What impressed me the most was that her work is not based solely on theory. It has been refined through 3 decades of counseling, research, and walking alongside people as they discovered that lasting change is possible.

Having now had the privilege of editing this manuscript, I can say with complete confidence that the same authenticity I witnessed years ago fills every chapter. The wisdom found in these pages is rooted in experience, supported by evidence, strengthened by faith, and presented with warmth, humility, and even humor.

Another impressive feature is Linda's unique ability to take complex concepts rooted in neuroscience, cognitive behavioral therapy, trauma recovery, and faith, and present them in a way that is accessible and immediately applicable. Too often, recovery books are either overly clinical or purely inspirational. Linda's work expertly finds the balance between the two.

Her "3 G Method" focusing daily on Gratitude, what you're Good at, and your Goal for the day, is a simple yet transformative framework. Backed by more than 35 years of professional counseling experience and a long history of success helping clients, her method is practical, memorable, and easy to implement.

What makes this book especially enjoyable is Linda's warmth and humor. She tackles serious topics like addiction, trauma, and broken relationships with honesty, an abundance of relatable stories, and plenty of heart. The book is filled with real-life examples of people who have overcome addiction, restored their marriages, revitalized their careers, and rebuilt their lives.

I also truly appreciated the book's interactive nature. Through journaling exercises, worksheets, and reflection questions, Linda encourages readers to do more than just read, she invites them to actively participate in their own healing journey.

Whether you are struggling with addiction, recovering from trauma, seeking spiritual growth, or simply searching for a practical way to improve your daily life, this book offers hope, direction, and a proven path forward. I highly recommend it to anyone ready to make meaningful changes—one day at a time.

Tammy Obermeier,
BS, Psychology
Certified Peer Specialist
Certified Recovery Coach
Neurolinguistic Practitioner and Life Coach

INDEX

INTRODUCTION

Let's be honest—if sheer willpower worked, we'd all be flawless, fabulous, and I would be fitting into those jeans from 1973, the house would always be clean, business would be booming and we would reach all our goals every day.

If you've been stuck in the same loop—starting fresh every Monday and falling apart by Wednesday (with snacks and a cocktail) it's not because you're lazy, crazy or broken. It's because you're using the wrong method.

You haven't yet been able to tap into the power of spirit filled habits by seeing yourself through God's eyes and His plan for you so I am going to give you my simple nutshell version of the 3 G system to reprogram your brain.

The truth is, Mind-Body-Spirit transformation doesn't come from sheer willpower. It takes using the 3 G method where you are practicing Gratitude, understanding and believing what God made you Good at, and setting and achieving Goals.

It's a no-nonsense, grace-filled, occasionally messy, and often hilarious (if you choose to laugh at yourself) path to real change.

This book isn't a shaming self help bootcamp with a rigid system to adhere to. It's more like a pep talk from your fun, slightly sarcastic online counselor, speaker, life coach, cheerleader who loves Jesus and also thinks you're amazing—even if you have totally different beliefs, fall on your proverbial face regularly, and come to our zoom coaching calls in your jammies without combing your hair.... It's all good. God loves you and so do I. No judgment.

If you stick with me you'll learn how to:

- Squeeze in spiritual growth without waking up at 4 a.m.
- Start your day with gratitude before your feet hit the floor
- Turn your gifts into goals instead of guilt trips
- Laugh at your mess while still cleaning it up
- Course-correct without driving in the muddy rut for miles on end
- And, actually enjoy the journey, even if the road is rocky and the construction leads you down an unknown path that takes you way longer than you had hoped.

WHY THE WEIRD BOOK STRUCTURE?

I have ADHD and I am getting older, I will be 71 this year. I know there are people like me out there who have probably never finished a book, or at least not recently, and can't remember three numbers in a row let alone all 10, I am making the chances a little bit better that you can actually get through this whole thing.

SHORT PARAGRAPHS

My husband just read a book by Trisha Fenimore called *Pray for Them* that was 500+ pages and when I opened it, I expected to have to climb Mount Everest, but nope almost every sentence was its own paragraph. Suddenly 500 pages felt like 50 and it made it so much easier to read so I decided to try it too.

A LOT OF HEADINGS

I usually read books to get some specific content, but I can never remember where it is in the book and it's really annoying so I am going to give you lots of headings so if you need to skim the book to find a particular thing you can do that.

BIG FONT and NOT TOO LONG

Most of us "seasoned folks" have bad eyes and shrinking attention spans so I'm keeping it easy to read, not just for us. but also for those other people who are on the spectrum. We're all on an alphabet soup spectrum of some sort like ADHD, OCD, GAD, MDD, BPD, LD, AODA and on and on!

EVERYDAY LANGUAGE

I want this to be understandable and easy to read for young people, and folks like me, who may not want to look up definitions every few pages because you don't know what the heck they are talking about.

This is for people who understand what words like stuff, yucky and a-bunch mean, and they aren't going to criticize the author for not using more intellectual words, or a million commas.

WHAT WOULD LINDA SAY ONE-LINERS

I got a laugh the first time one of my clients told me that "she heard my voice in her head" and it stopped her from saying something she would have regretted. Another client told me that she talked about me so much that when her husband would see her getting wound up he would say "What would Linda say?"

Today someone said "and then I heard my inner Linda voice, and I calmed down." I have requests for all kinds of products like talking bobble-heads, AI Apps, daily meditation pull cards or strips in jars to help them remember these tools, so that will be my next challenge!

But, in the meantime, I have written my one liners in big writing on pages all by themselves throughout the book.

The funny thing is that much of what I have learned, know and share comes from what Jesus or some other ancient guru said centuries ago which goes to show you that neurobiology, science and psychiatry have not come up with anything new, they are just proving that the teachings of old work.

RESCUE STORIES

I have been working with people for more than 40 years who come desperate for solutions to their problems. Since using the 3 G's I have witnessed some amazing successes so I included at least one in each chapter.

FOOD FOR THOUGHT REFLECTION QUESTIONS

My friend Becky suggested that I add a reflection section with questions so readers could take some time to journal their takeaways from the chapter, so you may want to get a journal or use the space provided as things come to mind.

TODAY IS THE DAY- LET'S DO THIS

This book will give you some concrete, simple, easy-brainer tools (it can't be a no-brainer because you really need to use your brain to get through this!)

So, whether you're rebooting your life, recovering from a detour, or just tired of circling the same emotional roundabout—the 3 G's are your permission slip to start over again and again with grace and hope.

Now grab your coffee, your journal, your Bible (if you are so inclined) and a pen because it's time to get growing.

PART I

CHAPTER 1:

HOW IT ALL BEGAN

THE KIDNEY STONE CHRONICLES & BIRTH OF THE 3 G'S

I never truly understood the power of gratitude, self-affirmation, and goal-setting until I faced a life-changing crisis in 2008.

While tragedy is undeniably painful, I have come to believe the truth of Romans 8:28: *"And we know that in all things God works for the good of those who love Him, who have been called according to His purpose."* Looking back, I realize that God had a plan for me all along, even if at the time I couldn't understand how it all fit together.

It all kicked off with a late-night phone call in April 2008. My dad was in the hospital, and they didn't know if he would live through the night.

My husband, Ralph, and I jumped into the car at 11 p.m. for the two-hour drive to Black River Falls, Wisconsin, and somewhere near the "middle of nowhere," Ralph winced in pain and announced, "It's another kidney stone."

Now, Ralph isn't your average kidney-stone sufferer. Oh no, he's a *collector*. Literally!! They are in a jar!

Over the years, this man has hosted more than 623 of these tiny devils in his body, which he describes as "imagine a porcupine doing the cha-cha through your internal plumbing."

When we finally arrived, we made a beeline for my dad's hospital room. After a few hugs, some tears, and a whispered prayer, we headed off to the emergency room—for Ralph this time.

Turns out, he had a 9mm kidney stone, which is apparently like trying to pass a marble through a straw. This one was not as challenging as the one in 2025 which was over 12mm and all total produced a quarry of 48 broken pieces in 3 weeks that he had to pee out through his... straw! LOL

I digress...back to the ER in Black River Falls. Surgery was in Ralph's future back then, but for the moment, he was given just enough pain medication to keep him from curling up in the corner crying like a baby, which I have actually seen him do.

The next morning, I entered my dad's room, and he was sleeping. I talked to my stepmom briefly, and then my dad opened his eyes, and he pointed into the corner of the room.

"Do you see them?" he asked in awe.

We looked into the corner, and there was nothing there.

I asked, "Dad, what do you see?"

"Look at them all!" He said.

I asked, "Dad, are you seeing the angels?"

"Yes," he said again, "look at them all!"

Tears welled up as I knew what was happening, so I asked, "Are they coming for you, Dad?"

He never really answered, but soon after the angel encounter, he closed his eyes, never spoke again, and within the hour, he was gone.

My dad was never an open book. He didn't share his feelings much yet when he spoke you knew it meant something. We never talked much about faith but I knew he believed, in part because he told us all a year earlier he was "ready to go."

Dad had cancer of the larynx and had undergone terribly painful radiation and had been reduced to nothing. He was merely sitting in the living room with a feeding tube in his stomach and a tube in his throat to help him speak. For months he was so doped up on pain medication "to keep him comfortable" during his end times that he couldn't function or care for himself.

Seeing him that way was heartbreaking. Fortunately after months of having to help him do everything, my brother advocated for a medication change. He started on Methadone and lived for almost a year walking, talking, doing self care and everything else until he got a bowel obstruction that finally took him.

This angel encounter was the most meaningful time I have had with my dad and it brought me great peace. We were closing the chapter on dad's time on this earth but life wasn't done throwing curveballs just yet.

THE SLIPPERY SLOPE TO ADDICTION

Over the next few months, Ralph became something of a regular in the operating room—three surgeries for kidney stones and one more to untwist his intestines after a bowel obstruction. Ironically, it was the same condition that had taken my father, so the experience was more than a little emotionally charged.

Ralph had been diagnosed with Crohn's disease back in 1978, and his relationship with his intestines could only be described as... complicated.

He'd lost 1.5 feet of them early on, including his ileum, then another foot in 2006, which subsequently led to an infection and a 58-day hospital stay. It was long enough for me to be such a fixture that I was making the staff coffee in the morning in their break room- and I am not joking!

In 2008, he underwent his most recent Crohn's surgery, and now he receives infusions every eight weeks to keep the Crohn's in check.

As if that wasn't enough, Ralph was also wrestling with chronic migraines (which he says are more painful than the kidney stones), sleep apnea, restless leg syndrome, arthritis, depression, and anxiety. He gets Vyepti infusions for that every 3 months and now will be doing botox treatments every 6 weeks to help migraines as well.

So here we are in September of 2008, and once again, he practically had his own designated surgical bed with nurses who were so invested that one of them, whose name was Chris, followed me out to the car one day and begged me to get him an implanted port to be able to access his veins more easily.

Chris was great at starting IVs, but between the nurses, the nurse anesthetist and the anesthesiologist, they had to poke him nine times to get an IV line before surgery, putting them an hour and a half behind schedule.

The next surgery was getting a port implanted, and it worked great for almost 10 years until he developed an infection and almost died. Since then, he has had 2 more implants that have been used hundreds of times since then.

CRASH LANDING ON THE BOTTOM OF THE SLIPPERY SLOPE

By this time it was October of 2008 when Ralph, without hesitation, blurted out, "I have something to tell you."

I waited.

"You aren't going to like it," he added.

Now Ralph is a generous guy. Even in the face of bankruptcy, he would give his last dollar to someone else.

We were struggling financially, and I figured he was going to say he had given someone something, but very matter-of-fact, he states, "I have been using."

"What do you mean?" I questioned. "How? When?"

"For a couple of months," he confessed.

I was really confused. I was with him, and I did not notice anything out of the ordinary.

Sure, he didn't feel well and had more days when he was tired or had pain, but what I didn't know is that he had been exaggerating his symptoms to get more medication, and when he did get it, he would take four or even six instead of two.

I was angry! My head was spinning along with my stomach!

"What are we going to do?" I pleaded with God for answers.

I had told Ralph when we got together in 1996 that if he used again, it was over, so what was I going to do? Divorce was no longer an option in my mind, but the "what ifs" overwhelmed me..

I was working full-time for the State of Wisconsin Job Center and spent another 20-30 hours a week helping to run the non-profit we had started, and I had no idea how I could possibly take over his responsibilities while doing everything else.

And what would people think that the director of this huge organization that everyone looked up to is now in a treatment center because he was addicted to narcotics? Despite my advocacy for getting rid of stigma, this one was hard.

I called around and found some places in Wisconsin for him to go that our insurance would have at least paid part of the cost, but he refused.

So now what do I do? Since I am a fix-it, get-it-done (and admittedly a recovering codependent) I was determined to figure it all out.

We had been watching the TV show called "Intervention," and he said he wanted to go to Pacific Hills Christian Treatment Center in California.

I called and got things set up, and within a week, he was on a plane. It cost us $25,000 and a lot of emotional ups and downs on our journey to experiencing a change that would transform our lives and millions of other people all over the world for all eternity.

It was at Pacific Hills Christian Treatment Center (now known as Covenant Hills), that Ralph discovered the miracle of starting each day with the "3 G's"- practicing Gratitude, writing what you are Good at, and setting Goals, so every day since Ralph returned home in November of 2008, we have used the 3 G's with the residents in our sober houses and thousands of other people all over the world.

3 Gs OF GRATITUDE
GRATITUDE
THANKFUL FOR:
WHAT I'M GOOD AT
MY TALENTS & STRENGTHS
GOALS
REACH FOR THE STARS
MOVING FORWARD

THE EFFECT

Another blessing Ralph got when he was in treatment was being able to attend a recovery church called "The Effect," where Dave Brisbin was the pastor. Almost all of the people that went there were in recovery and it was the most peaceful, uplifting church we had ever been to.

We still listen to Dave's sermons on YouTube, and it so happens that we just listened to the one he uploaded today about gratitude. Now that is what we call "a God thing!" To bring us a sermon by Dave on the day we are writing a chapter on gratitude and visiting his church 18 years ago is a real blessing!

Dave has written some great books himself! I interviewed him about *Daring to Think Again: Restoring Jesus' Original Challenge to the Faith We Think We Know,* and it is amazing.

In his message on gratitude today he was talking about a fellow author, Rich Rohr, who wrote in *The Universal Christ*, page 63, that "Brain studies have shown that we may be hardwired to focus on problems at the expense of a positive vision. The human brain wraps around fear and problems like Velcro."

He goes on to say "We dwell on bad experiences long after the fact, and spend vast amounts of energy anticipating what might go wrong in the future. Conversely, positivity and gratitude and simple happiness slide away like cheese on hot Teflon."

This is so true, and I am going to try to help you reprogram your brain so your happiness isn't slipping away with your negative thoughts like our Wisconsin cheese does on those Teflon pans!

IMPORTANT TOXIC TEFLON DIGRESSION

My Pastor thought I might want to change "Teflon" to non-stick pans because he feared you young pups may not have heard of Teflon. I laughed then realized I am old enough to be his mother so maybe I just need to do the old lady mom/grandma thing and explain that Teflon was a product they use to put on pans that they later determined would cause toxic fumes and cause "Teflon Flu" if it got scratched or heated too hot. It was taken off the market in 2014.

Back to the mission of the book…I am writing this so that you can focus on the positive things in life instead of getting stuck on the negative thoughts that steal the joy from your life and hinder you from being all God wants you to be.

Here is the first of many rescue stories that have come from the power of the 3 G's.

RESCUE STORY #1 – CATHY, THE PHYSICAL THERAPIST

Cathy contacted us inquiring about the sober house that we had. She stated that she was a professional and was moving to our community and needed a sober house.

I had circumvented numerous scammers with big stories about being doctors and lawyers wanting to come and just board at our house, so I wasn't buying it, but she kept calling back until I realized she was serious. She was very aware she needed help.

Cathy had been struggling with her alcohol abuse for a couple of years and was in and out of treatment. She had lost her job because of her drinking and finally hit bottom. She was able to get another job, but she was very afraid she would blow it if she kept drinking and she didn't know how to stop.

It was a roller coaster for her for over a year. As a professional with a master's degree, like me, she had a really hard time accepting that as smart as she was, she did not have the wherewithal to quit drinking.

She rationalized that she was a 30 year old woman and had come this far and was smart enough to decide to have a few drinks when she wanted and not have it be a problem. Unfortunately, for whatever reason, she just couldn't do it.

She couldn't even stay sober in sober houses with supervision, so she had to go to a more restrictive environment that was more interactive and supportive.

Taking one day at a time, accepting her addiction as it was and changing perspectives on life using things like the 3 G's, finding her purpose in a job she enjoyed, and getting the support from others, she was able to quit alcohol for good.

It has been over 10 years and she is working, she bought a house, got a new car, and feels good about her sobriety.

She still struggles with depression and anxiety at times but she has the tools now, like the 3 G's, and people in recovery to get her through the tough times. She also has come to accept that she is smart and she has the choice to drink but for her, it is not an option.

IT'S A CHOICE BUT NOT AN OPTION

THE MIND/BODY/SPIRIT BENEFIT OF THE 3 G'S IN A NUTSHELL

I am going to go into much more detail later in the book on how the scientific and medical evidence as well as how the spiritual aspect (with some Bible references) will show how these 3 habits work.

In the meantime, I want to give you an overview of what is going on in the brain and why the 3 G's are worth your time to start immediately.

When we practice gratitude, self-affirmation, or goal-setting, we're all using many of the same "higher" parts of the brain. The front of the brain, called the prefrontal cortex, is especially important.

You can think of it as your inner CEO, planner, and spiritual director all rolled into one. Any time you pause to notice what you're thankful for, remind yourself of your strengths, or think about where you want your life to go, this front region is working hard.

Another shared system is the brain's reward and motivation network. When you feel a sense of appreciation, pride, or excitement about a goal, your brain releases chemicals that say, "Hey, this is good—let's do more of this," which is your built-in reward program without the subscription fee. Even though they overlap, each practice leans on the brain in a slightly different way.

Gratitude tends to light up areas involved in feeling connected and safe. When you recognize something good you've received—from life, from another person, or from God—your brain shifts attention away from threat and scarcity toward a sense of provision.

It's like switching from the "Breaking News" channel in your head (where everything is an emergency) to a quiet nature documentary reminding you that some things are still beautiful. This not only boosts mood but also calms stress-related regions that keep you in fight-or-flight mode.

In simple terms, gratitude tells your brain, "You're not as alone or as deprived as you feel," which softens anxiety and resentment and gives your nervous system a chance to stop acting like there's a lion under the dining room table.

What you are Good at (Self-Affirmation) on the other hand, focuses more on the brain's sense of identity. When you tell yourself, "I am capable," "I am learning," or "I am loved," regions that process self-relevant information go to work. These areas help hold together the story you tell about who you are.

If your inner dialogue has been harsh or shame-filled, affirmations give your brain new material to work with—like updating the script from a tragedy to a redemption story.

When first practicing self-affirmations, your brain might respond, "Wait, we don't usually say nice things in here," but with repetition, those kinder lines start to feel more familiar.

Over time, this can reduce the power of old, negative beliefs and make it easier to face challenges without immediately jumping to, "I'm a failure; please bring snacks."

Goal-setting leans more heavily on the brain's planning and self-control systems. When you set a clear goal—anything from "I'm going to cut back on drinking" to "I want to run a 5K"—the parts of your brain that organize steps, hold plans in mind, and resist temptations become more engaged.

These regions help you break a big intention into smaller actions and stick with them, even when the couch and a bowl of chips make a very persuasive counteroffer.

With repetition, the brain's habit circuits begin to take over, making it more automatic to act in ways that support your goals.

Eventually, your brain starts saying, "This is just what we do now," instead of treating every good decision like a special event.

So while gratitude, self-affirmation, and goals all draw on similar brain networks for attention, meaning, and motivation, they emphasize different questions.

Gratitude asks, "What is good right now?"

Good at (self-affirmation) asks, "Who am I, really?"

Goals ask, "Where am I going, and what do I need to do next?"

Together, they give the brain a powerful trio: a calmer view of the present, a kinder view of the self, and a clearer path into the future—with just enough cooperation from your brain that you don't have to bribe it with coffee every five minutes.

THE CHALLENGE- YOUR TURN

If you are reading this book, I hope it is because you are seeking, on some level, to consider how you can enjoy life more by gaining some tools to do it.

If so, please join us in the transformation now by grabbing a pen and a journal or opening a Google Doc and your microphone, and start by making a comprehensive list of everything you can think of to answer these questions.

1. What am I grateful for?
2. What am I good at? (Yes, you're allowed to brag a little and ask others to help you!.)
3. What are my goals?

And tonight, you reflect on these:

1. What am I grateful for that happened today?
2. What good things did I do that made a difference?
3. What goals did I achieve?

Oh, and one critical rule—no negativity before bed. If you're tempted to slap a "but" on your accomplishments, I'll personally sign you up for my patented "Butectomy" course, where we will surgically remove that toxic vocabulary (metaphorically).

WARNING-Side effects of the butectomy include uncontrollable positivity and occasional bursts of self-confidence and accomplishment of goals like you have never done before. That means no "I did this, BUT..." nonsense.

By keeping it simple and staying consistent, the 3 G's can rewire your brain, reconnect you to your body and your spirit, and help you rediscover hope—even when life feels like a soap opera written by a sadistic scriptwriter.

The rest of this book will unpack why the 3 G's work—scientifically, spiritually, and practically- and if Ralph and I can survive everything we have, so can you.

Buckle up, Let's do this!

FOOD FOR THOUGHT

1. What is the main thing you got out of this chapter?

2. What are the top 3 things that come to your mind that you are grateful for?

3. What are the top 3 things that come to your mind that you are good at?

4. What are the top 3 goals that come to mind that are causing you stress that you will start (or stop) doing now?

JOURNALING THE 3 G's and MORE

THOUGHTS CAUSE FEELINGS AND FEELINGS CAUSE BEHAVIORS

CHAPTER 2:

INTRODUCTION TO THE TOXIC THOUGHT COCKTAIL

WHAT ARE YOU THINKING ABOUT RIGHT NOW?

Is it something deep and meaningful… or is it chocolate?

Why do you THINK you chose this book to read at this particular time in your life? Was it destiny? A profound inner calling that led you to buy it… or did it just have a cool cover and wasn't buried under a pile of laundry like the other one you have been meaning to read for the last year or two?

What do you THINK you will use it for? Personal growth? Life-changing wisdom? Learning how to get sober or lose weight? Or perhaps as a coaster for your coffee?

Our thoughts have incredible power—they can build us up or break us down. They can encourage or discourage, empower or weaken, heal or harm.

Basically, thoughts are like my husband with the remote control when one minute he is watching Gunsmoke and then to NCIS and then it's Touched by an Angel and then the WWE. For those of you who don't know what that is, the WWE is the World Wrestling Entertainment, where people do incredibly insane and painful things to each other because millions of people love to watch it!

Then, after all that channel changing, he ramps up the pain by ending on a political news station that is enough to push me over the edge!

So NOW what are you thinking about? Is it the strange combination of shows that he watches or why people enjoy watching people hurt each other, or if angels are real?

Or, perhaps you are wondering if he watches Fox News or MSNBC so you can draw some conclusion as to whether or not he's one of "those" people who share fake news, or propaganda.

Or, maybe you are thinking about whether or not that first paragraph was actually one sentence and now I am cheating on my promise to keep things short?

Our minds go where they are led unless we decide to take charge of them and give our thoughts direction because thoughts cause feelings and feelings cause behavior...be it good or bad, you decide.

I know that is not an easy task for most of us, and we literally have to reprogram our brains to do it, but it is possible. I have found some great reminders in a really good book my mom and dad introduced me to very early in my childhood. They used to sing me to sleep with a song about it- I am sure you have heard it- "Jesus loves me this I know, for the Bible tells me so."

I hung on to that basic tenet of the Christian faith and though I did little with it until I was in my twenties, I have since found a great deal of wisdom in it and I have done my best to love others as I believed that the Jesus I came to know does, and I hope you can see some of the benefit as I share it.

Paul, for example, was kind of a feisty disciple and didn't pull any punches when he wrote letters to the different churches. He didn't always get resounding applause when he told them what they needed to do if they wanted to follow Jesus.

I love what he said in the book of Romans when he gave them a directive (notice I said directive, not suggestion). Chapter 12:2 says, "Do not be conformed to this world, but be transformed by the renewal of your mind, that by testing, you may discern what is the will of God, what is good and acceptable and perfect."

What that means to me is that God came up with a whole bunch of good instructions to keep our thoughts heading in a positive direction so we can have the life He meant for us to have and be a good example to others.

I've been working to figure that out for the last 50 years, and what I have found is that the 3G's is a super simple practice that has done more for me and my clients, friends, and family than anything else I ever learned in graduate school, bible college, or anyplace else.

Did you grab your notebook or journal yet, or did you already forget? It will help you to stay focused (that is, if you actually use it and write stuff down!), and if you do this every day, I promise it will help your life, and you will reach more goals than you ever thought possible.

HOW I USE THE 3 G'S AND WHY

Every day I post my 3 G's in our private Facebook group, and today I wrote-

"I am GRATEFUL that God has given me the desire and ability to write this book."

"I am GOOD at sharing my thoughts in somewhat of an understandable and humorous way that seems to resonate with others."

"My GOAL is to write another 7,000 words today, quit second-guessing myself and just have fun."

Why am I writing this book? It is definitely NOT for the money. Contrary to popular belief, your average, run-of-the-mill author doesn't exactly swim in piles of cash; in fact, we'd be lucky to wade ankle-deep.

My mission in life isn't about stacking dollars, but it's about changing lives for the better. I think that's why God created me, (and you as well) and for me, I have honestly found that following what I think He wants me to do has worked out pretty well for me so far, so I figure—why change what's working?

I choose to believe that God had something to do with you picking up this book and if it makes you smile at least once, makes your life a little better, your mental health a little less annoying, or your addictive tendencies a little less intense, then mission accomplished, and it has been worth every second of time, effort, brainpower, and money that I've invested.

I'm writing this because what I have to say *works*. Technically speaking, each of the 3 G's have been part of Cognitive Behavioral Therapy (CBT) and Neuro Linguistic Programming (NLP) strategies that scientists call "evidence-based practices," for many years.

Gratitude, self-affirmation, and goal setting have proven results as you will see in the references I offer in this book, but the thing that is different about the 3 G's is how they work together as a process or system that, when integrated, work in a more powerful way and can be used all day long with everything you do.

Check out my next rescue story and you will see what I mean.

RESCUE STORY #2 JULIE – THE 3RD GRADE TEACHER

Julie was a young elementary school teacher who had not been in the profession for very long. She had always wanted to be a teacher, but had no idea the challenges she would face. When she came to me for counseling, she stated she would cry from Sunday all the way through until Monday when she had to drag herself to work nauseous and stressed.

She would have panic attacks, difficulty sleeping and eating, and was beginning to hate the job, primarily because of Johnny. He was defiant, rebellious, hyperactive, and negative, and he brought a toxicity to the classroom that permeated everything.

She had tried everything to manage his behavior, and she had to admit, she simply did not like this boy, and she felt very guilty and like a complete failure as a teacher.

I encouraged her to begin doing the 3 G's for herself every day to gain confidence, and then I suggested she bring it to school. She did just that!

She started on Sunday saying things like "I am grateful I am a teacher and get to help children learn.

I am good at showing up and doing my best. Goal is to use the 3 G's to stay positive and help the children learn it."

She started every morning when the children had their morning circle time, she had them go around and share what they were grateful for, what they were good at, and what they wanted to get done that day.

Sometimes the children would get stuck and couldn't think of what to say, so she encouraged the other children to offer some ideas to them when they got stuck. By the end of that first week, she came back to me astounded by the change it had made.

Some of these children had never heard anybody say they were good at anything, especially Johnny. But when the other children, and Johnny, started looking for the good in one another, and he heard them compliment him on things, he became the first one to tell another child what they were good at.

His leadership was negative in the past because that's the way he got attention. She realized he had developed a "muddy rut of toxic waste self-talk" that she was able to help him reprogram through the 3G strategy. (More on the muddy rut analogy later.)

Sometimes our mind will tell us that negative attention is better than no attention. We probably noticed it when the kids were little. Clearly, positive attention is a much better way to develop self-efficacy, cooperation and motivation. The key is, if you want to get good at something, it has to be practiced over and over again.

I only worked with Julie for a couple of months, but by then Johnny was leading the children to the lunchroom and was one of the most positive students in her classroom because that's the one thing he could do right is be a strong leader that other kids came to like and she realized she was a great teacher that could change lives in powerful ways.

Hmm... this is interesting!
What can I learn from this?

MY "WHERE AM I?" BRAIN TRANSFORMATION JOURNEY

When I look back at my own journey of transformation, I had to face what my behavior was costing me and if I needed to consider this whole mind/brain/body/spirit changing decision.

It was 1976. One minute, I was all decked out in my hip-hugger bell-bottom jeans, the big gold peace belt, my tie-dyed halter top, and my leather jacket with fringes, saying, "Wow, man, this is groovy. Pass me that pot pipe and pour me another glass of wine."

The next thing I know, I'm waking up saying, "Where am I? Who are you? How did I get here? "

The fear of not knowing where I was and who these people were, and worse, what I had done that I didn't remember, caused such guilt and shame that by the end of the day, I am asking myself, "What the heck is wrong with me? I can't seem to quit any of this. I am worthless, a horrible person, and maybe I should just kill myself."

Do you see the rollercoaster of thoughts that caused my feelings, which led to behavior? That is always the process.

It was a 16-year-old girl from a wonderful Christian family who shared something radical with me. She said: "Linda, there's a way to be mentally healthy without relying on unhealthy crutches like alcohol, drugs, or other addictions."

WOW…who knew?

I realized I'd been living in my own personal hell, addicted not just to alcohol and drugs, but to pretty much anything else the '70s had to offer. (And trust me, the '70s had *plenty* to offer—sex, drugs, rock 'n' roll,and questionable fashion choices, which, by the way, the clothes are all back in style again and I get compliments on them!)

That was my spiritual awakening. She handed me a Bible and showed me how to look up scriptures based on what I was feeling—guilt, hurt, loneliness, shame. It was like a divine Google search, long before the internet existed.

While technology is great, there's no substitute for talking to an actual human who's experienced the wisdom of the Bible, the love of Jesus, the power of the Holy Spirit, and the grace of God firsthand and who has demonstrated that neuroplasticity is a real thing and you can reprogram your brain with the spirit-mind-body connection.

So that's why I'm here. I was a mess. Now I'm much less of a mess. I'm not perfect—none of us are—but I've traded the panic button that I used to push back in those days, followed by a stiff drink, for my Bible and a 3 G's journal that starts with Gratitude.

I no longer gasp, "OMG, what am I going to do? This is awful! This isn't fair!" Instead, 95% of the time, I look at life's curveballs and say, "Hmm... this is interesting! What can I learn from this, Lord?"

These moments are what I call AFGOs: **A**nothe**r** **F**lipping **G**rowth **O**pportunity. In case you are wondering, yes, I changed the F word from the original version my friend Sally shared.

Besides being more socially acceptable, I learned in gymnastics that if you are "flipping," whether forward or backward, you are shifting perspective the entire time. Sure, sometimes you fall on your face but it's all part of learning how to navigate the task before you.

So, welcome to my AFGO-filled journey. I hope it helps you with yours.

The next few chapters will give you scientific evidence and an understanding of how this spirit brain transformation actually works, so you can practice the verse we talked about earlier... Romans 12:2 "Don't be conformed to this world but be transformed by the renewing of your mind."

AFGO
"Another Flipping
Growth
Opportunity"

FOOD FOR THOUGHT

1. What is the main thing you got out of this chapter?

___

___

___

2. What do you think your mission or purpose is on this earth?

___

___

___

3. What negative thoughts or behaviors come to mind that limit you from living your purpose?

___

___

___

4. What action can you take today to get unstuck?

___

___

___

JOURNALING THE 3 G's and MORE

___

___

___

___

___

___

___

___

___

CHAPTER 3:

DON'T THINK ABOUT THAT- THE MIND-BODY CONNECTION

In her book *Who Switched Off My Brain? Controlling Toxic Thoughts and Emotions, (2009 and* 2013), Dr. Caroline Leaf reveals "research shows that 87% of illnesses can be attributed to our thought life and approximately 13% to diet, genetics, and environment."

The likelihood you will find others making those same claims is slim, but the reality is, if you think about it, our thoughts do quite a number on us everyday. Granted, it isn't necessarily thoughts in and of themselves but how those thoughts are interpreted and what we do with them that leads us into self-sabotaging our health.

Think about it this way; our thoughts are like the steering wheel of your day. When you park them in "what if?" and "why me?" mode, your feelings quickly follow—fear, anger, stress and anxiety revs the engine, and soon we are barreling toward panic, depression or resentment and then the transmission goes haywire and we are either stuck in neutral or going backwards!

Then your body starts acting out the script: headaches that won't quit, stomach knots that feel like they have a personality, and that sluggish, worn-down "something is off" feeling that never seems to fully lift and the mechanic has no openings to fix your broken transmission!

Emotions aren't just in the brain; they're a complex interaction between brain activity, chemical signals, and physical sensations throughout your body, influencing behavior and vice versa.

Spirituality is also a factor in our brain chemistry as well and we will talk about how a healthy spiritual connection can positively impact this connection in future chapters. In fact, God can be the best mechanic, or surgeon you have dealt with and He is on call 24/7!

Many brain and neurology experts and researchers support what Dr. Leaf explains in her book:

"The brain is an extremely complex neuroplastic responder. This essentially means that each time it's stimulated by your mind, it responds in many different ways, including neurochemical, genetic, and electromagnetic changes. This, in turn, grows and changes structures in the brain, building or wiring in new physical thoughts." she says.

In other words, we can change our minds (I am grateful instead of miserable) which will change our brains, and create a new neural pathway! Whether our thoughts are good or bad is up to us.

No matter what happens, we must understand that we can choose what we think about and how we respond to our experiences.

You have to ask yourself, "Do I want this 'thing' to become a memory that will linger in my brain for the rest of my life and keep me stuck in a loop of nauseous roller coaster emotions, or not?"

For me... I say NO! But it is not that easy...we need each other to keep this in mind!

WHERE DOES ALL THIS BRAIN STUFF START?

Now this section may be a bit much for those of you who don't care about studies and statistics and such, but for the sake of credibility to my claims, I thought I would share it anyway.

Here are some astounding facts from a book featured on the National Institute of Health (NIH) website called *Discovering the Brain.*

"The brain starts developing at the tip of a 3mm neural tube and must grow at a rate of 250,000 nerve cells a minute to arrive at the more than 100 trillion neurons by the time the baby is born."

As the research shows, our brains can be reprogrammed by rerouting the neural pathways. The NIH defines neuroplasticity as "the ability of the nervous system to change its activity in response to intrinsic or extrinsic stimuli by reorganizing its structure, functions, or connections."

This is really good news because there are a lot of things that cause problems with our brains from the moment we are conceived. It could be traumatic events, environmental toxins, foods we eat, things we drink, and, even what we think.

So, let me give you a quick overview of how we have been impacted since the time we were conceived and what we can do about it today.

CHILDHOOD INFLUENCERS

As we all know, mom and dad bring a whole slew of chemical chaos into the mix of how our brains and bodies function. Genetic pros and cons from mom and dad fill us from one proverbial end to the other, and some of it we can change, and some of it, not so much.

Something that impacts us from the get-go is the environment in which we were conceived. And the one we spent the first nine months floating in, being fed without having to cook a meal ourselves! Wouldn't that be nice today?

The bad part is that if mom is drinking alcohol and smoking cigarettes and doing drugs and eating junk food (or no food), we may be born with a low birth weight, fetal alcohol syndrome, addiction to drugs, and other types of brain damage.

The National Childhood Traumatic Stress Network (NCTSN) research has shown "An absence of mental stimulation in neglectful environments may limit the brain from developing to its full potential. Children with complex trauma histories may develop chronic or recurrent physical complaints, such as headaches or stomachaches."

If they have not received enough interaction, they may develop a detachment disorder and are not able to bond not only with a parent, but with others, which may impact the rest of their lives if they don't get help to reprogram their brains.

Unfortunately, many of these children may develop illnesses like anxiety disorders, depression, obsessive-compulsive disorder, oppositional-defiant disorder, or other mental illnesses that impact their futures in a variety of ways.

Studies on children who developed oppositional defiant disorder (ODD) were found to often have had experiences like a chaotic or dysfunctional family life, inconsistent parenting, lack of parental supervision, and exposure to abuse or neglect.

Often there were socioeconomic factors that may have been related to exposure to violence or substance abuse and negative peer influences that led to antisocial behavior or addictive behaviors.

Clearly, brain development and functioning are scientifically, medically, and genetically connected to how we live our lives each day, who we live them with, and how we interact and perceive things.

So what do we do to make sure that our brains are taken care of and we are heading in the right direction in life?

Get rid of the rotten potatoes in your mind before your whole life stinks

THE TREE AND THE ROTTEN POTATO

As you probably noticed by now, I love analogies, parables, and visualizations because they stick in my brain better, so here is another one that my clients have used and have found to be a great tool when they start that stinking thinking.

Now think about an apple tree… or whatever other plant type you may want to grow for food. What do you need to make sure you get something edible that looks good, smells good, and tastes good?

You start with soil, right? And then you add some fertilizer, and then you water it. Add some warm sunlight, and you have a recipe for a great crop.

But, you can't just do it once; you have to keep feeding it and keep watering it because it is the food and water and good soil and sunshine that make everything work together to bring the nutrients through the roots all the way through every limb, every branch, and every seed that creates a flower that creates the food.

This same process goes on in our bodies. For us humans, our brains are fed by what goes into our bellies, and then our brain processes the food and tells all of our vital organs what to do with it.

It is quite fascinating when you think about it, which, unfortunately, we often don't. In fact, we are often downright mindless when it comes to what we are putting into our bodies.

Sitting on the couch watching TV with a mega bag of chips, and you end up wondering who came in while you were engrossed in the program, and ate them all! And we pay the price.

For example, the US obesity rate in 2017-2018 indicates a major public health concern, with 82.3% of adults classified as overweight a Body Mass Index (BMI) over 30 according to the "National Health and Nutritional Examination Survey.

Obesity is a major contributor to many of the leading causes of death. In 2023, it included heart disease, cancer, accidents (unintentional injuries), chronic lower respiratory diseases, Alzheimer's disease, diabetes, nephritis, chronic liver disease and cirrhosis, and COVID-19.

As you see, one of the diseases is liver disease and cirrhosis of the liver, which are primarily caused by excessive alcohol consumption and obesity. Since I work largely with alcoholics, and going along with my analogy of our bodies being like a plant, I got to thinking about what happens to a plant if you water it with vodka, so just for fun, I googled it!

According to "Green Citizen" - an environmental conservation company providing the world with information, services, and products to help live a sustainable life, shared this study.

- Dehydration and wilting: Alcohol can cause plants to lose water rapidly, leading to dehydration and wilting.
- Stunted growth: Studies have shown that even diluted alcohol solutions can stunt the growth of plant stems. (CBS News report)
- Root damage and nutrient absorption problems: High concentrations of alcohol can be toxic to plant roots, hindering their ability to absorb water and essential nutrients.
- Leaf damage and yellowing: High ethanol levels can stress plants, leading to leaf damage, browning, and yellowing.
- Death: If the alcohol concentration is high enough or the plant is repeatedly watered with vodka, it can be fatal to the plant. Solutions greater than 10% alcohol can be particularly damaging.

Our bodies are the same. We need healthy nutrients and water to thrive if we are going to produce the fruit of healthy brains and bodies that we desire.

WARNING...For you rationalizing alcoholics who are thinking "no worries, I don't drink vodka, I just drink beer," the same thing will happen with other kinds of alcoholic beverages also. Good try though! LOL

BEER
VODKA
WARNING- Alcohol is not food

THE CHALLENGE OF MINDFULNESS

In thousands of research studies, scientists have discovered that there are billions of actions that are going on in the brain at any one time of which we are only conscious of a fraction of them.

Think about it. We don't tell our heart to beat, our lungs to breathe, our blood to flow, or our joints to ache but when we learn to use our minds, we can tell our brain to slow the heartbeat, manage the pain, lower our blood pressure, and so much more.

Those things that we are aware of are now part of the trillions of experiences that are somewhere in our memory banks. The key is, are we focusing on the positive experiences or the negative?

I consider the positive experiences to be like beautiful, tasty apples on our brain tree. Happy thought apples that we can choose to enjoy. You pick them, you think about them, you remember them, and they create more positive neural pathways that kick off wonderful chemicals and bring you a sense of peace and love. (hmm..are apples honestly my happy thoughts? Or, is it chocolate cake with peanut butter frosting?... I digress!)

If you are having a really great day and all of a sudden something happens, like you get put down by your boss or a loved one, you blow a tire and are late for work, you see something bad on the news, someone cancels plans you were really looking forward to, or someone ate the last of the ice cream and didn't tell you?

Tell me if I'm wrong, but what happens? I am guessing your thoughts and peace of mind have gone out the window and you are focusing on whatever bugged you the most?

All of a sudden, just one of those negative events becomes more like a rotten potato. It smells so bad that you throw the whole bag away.

To be honest, most people don't pour the smelly bag of potatoes into a sink and rinse all of them off to see which one is the bad one. Neither do most of us sort through our thoughts to get rid of the bad ones and keep the good ones.

When we are facing negative emotions, most of us take the easy way out because we have to face the yucky painful stuff and decide to let it go in order to refocus on the good stuff.

So instead of facing the negative thoughts and dealing with them we complain to others about it over and over again thinking that will help. We ruminate on it, and every time we do that, we're creating a new memory that gets re-stuck in the memory banks of our subconscious minds.

This whole process creates toxic chemicals in our brain that, in turn, negatively impact those neural pathways. It causes us mental and physical illnesses and literally damages our brains.

Not only are we not throwing the rotten potato away, but we are also eating the darn thing and it's making us sick!

Are you ready to face the rotten potatoes that you have in your brain and get them out of the toxic neural pathways that you are stuck in? Is forgiveness the answer? Is letting go of what you can't control the key? More on these thoughts later... In the meantime, check out this next success story.

RESCUE STORY #3 JOE – FROM MARINE TO TREATMENT CENTER TO SOBER HOUSE OWNER

Joe had been a Marine for more than 15 years and loved his military service, despite the trauma that he saw that he didn't realize had caused some damaged neural pathways and toxic ways of thinking about how the world should be and how people should act.

He had a successful professional career until the toxic place he worked got the best of him and he started using alcohol to cope.

It started out with a couple drinks after work but it eventually spiraled right into a treatment center. After realizing he needed help he decided to try our Randlin Homes Reintegration Assistance Program.

Joe's health had deteriorated significantly, as well as his confidence. Surprisingly, he did still have a driver's license and being a natural leader, he was put in charge of driving a moving truck and overseeing the crew to pick up and deliver donated goods for the training program's secondhand store.

The whole point of the 3 G's is to build confidence and develop a new path in your brain. Joe did this, and instead of being hopeless, he realized that he had value, he had purpose, and he was making a difference again in a variety of ways.

His leadership skills were noticed, and he was given the opportunity to be a mentor in one of the sober houses. He continued on for several years, volunteering or getting a minimal stipend to add to his military benefits as well as free housing for his service to the other residents.

Eventually, he got a job and very quickly rose to become the employee of the month. He continued to work and save money while residing as a mentor in one of the houses.

After 11 years involved with the program, he remained clean and sober, and when we decided to retire from operating that home, we offered Joe the opportunity to purchase it, and he did.

It took a long time but Joe quit beating himself up for needing to get help with where things had spiraled down to, but he kept on being Grateful for his progress, realizing what he was Good at and setting Goals for the future.

It has been nearly four years since then, and his sober home is flourishing and he even has people on a waiting list to get in!

It was hard, but this marine learned to be Grateful to be living in a sober house, having people tell him what to do when he wasn't even getting paid to be there, but he eventually learned it was a real blessing.

He learned that he was still in service to his country by helping other alcoholics and drug addicts to start over and realize their value in the world. His confidence grew until he believed in himself once again to take the step to own his own sober house. He could fill out the "what am I Good at" list with ease.

He had reached the Goal of having a great life after the military and had learned the miracle of positive self-talk and reprogramming your brain so that you can do far more than you imagined.

This could be you! Are you ready to make a change and become what you know you could be? Are you ready to learn to get comfortable with your uncomfortable life?

WE HAVE TO GET
COMFORTABLE
BEING UNCOMFORTABLE

FOOD FOR THOUGHT SECTION:

1. What are the rotten potatoes you have in your brain that you need to get rid of?

   ____
   ____
   ____

2. What areas of your life could you be more mindful?

   ____
   ____
   ____

3. What behaviors come to mind that limit you from living your purpose?

   ____
   ____
   ____

4. What action can you take today to get unstuck?

   ____
   ____
   ____

JOURNALING THE 3 G's and MORE

____
____
____
____
____
____
____
____
____
____

CHAPTER 4:

THE BRAIN AND BODY ON TRAUMA

TRAUMA DOESN'T HAVE TO DESTROY YOU

I'm writing this chapter on the coast of South Carolina where we have gone for the 2nd year in a row to rest, relax and reset mentally, spiritually and physically.

This year we had to take a different route because in September of 2024 a catastrophic hurricane changed the landscape and residents forever.

Entire towns, and many of their residents are still buried under the debris. The trauma this caused will live deep underground, literally, and also in the hearts and souls of all those who have been affected.

They are having to rebuild everything from scratch and create new roads because the ones they had were so damaged that it was too dangerous to travel down them.

That is exactly what all of us who have experienced trauma need to do with our brains and I believe we all have experienced trauma in one way or another. It could be an illness, a death, something we have heard, seen or even done that was traumatizing at that moment.

In order to get out of the muddy rut of trauma, negativity, stress, anxiety, depression, anger and resentment, we need to forge a new path. The challenge is that we have to choose to build it with new thoughts.

I have found that contacting "the big guy upstairs" who originally created my neural pathways, to help re-route them, is the only way to do it right. He already gave us an entire "how to" manual, so I will share more of that with you later!

TRAUMA CAN BRING UNITY

Whether it's a natural disaster, a traumatic event, a pandemic, a financial crisis, or other tragedy, people are resilient and it really warms my heart to see how people step up to help each other. In fact, a study by Sae Hwang Han from The University of Texas at Austin, tracked over 30,000 adults for two decades and found that people who regularly help others experience 15-20% slower cognitive decline as they age.

The researchers concluded that we seem to be wired to benefit from acts of service, creating a biological reward system for doing good. I believe that for the majority of us, that innate sense of compassion is awakened and we desire to help.

When people were involved in mass shootings, floods, fires, pandemics or other natural disasters around the world, it doesn't matter whose child or loved one they were, if they were legal citizens or not, what color they were, or what political party or faith they belonged to, people reached out to help.

Today, in my hometown of Wausau, Wisconsin on day 35 of the 2026 government shutdown businesses and churches are offering free food to "anyone who needs it." They aren't checking "eligibility." they are saying if you have need "come…receive" No questions asked.

There is an African proverb, likely originating from the Nigerian Igbo culture, one of the largest and most influential ethnic groups in Africa, that says "It takes a village to raise a child." If we could only get beyond our selfishness to look at those that God has created and put right in front of us as our privilege to serve, we would have a lot fewer problems because in God's kingdom there are no walls.

Clearly when tragedy happens, it innately triggers the 3 G's in our brains to change the neural pathways from selfish, judgmental anger toward others to compassion where we are now seeing what to be grateful for (we are not in crises) what we are good at (helping others) and our goals (to do something) and suddenly we feel better!

Read on for more on how that happens!

ABOUT THOSE NEURAL PATHWAYS-NEW ANALOGY- THE MUDDY RUT

When I was growing up on the farm we had a long dirt driveway and in the spring it was a challenge to get up it with my little car.

Like toxic thoughts, it was pulling me in ways that I had no control over at times. Most of the time I could maneuver it and get up that quarter mile driveway until my dad would drive up with the milk truck and put a trench so deep I would immediately get pulled into the muddy rut and get stuck.

Every negative thought you think, and bad experience that happens, gets thrown into this muddy rut (a neural pathway.) The more toxic negative things there are in your brain, the deeper and more toxic the neural pathway becomes.

So what happens with toxic waste in nature? It goes deep underground and pollutes everything and eventually some things get sick or die.

Even when a bulldozer comes and pushes the dirt over the toxic garbage you have thrown into those muddy ruts, the junk that was deep down in that rut is just covered up with new dirt, it's not really gone.

It may not surface for years, if ever, but it is lurking somewhere inside us and even when we don't realize it, toxic mental waste is poisoning us and keeping us stuck in patterns of resentment, anger, pain, depression, anxiety and much more.

The deeper the "rut" the more it is hidden in the recesses of our minds seeping deep into our subconscious minds. As enough time passes we may not even recall it until a trigger happens.

It could be “a flood” of events that has now exposed what’s underneath and it brings this toxic waste to the surface to knock you around like an upended tree after a hurricane.

When we think about the acts of kindness and why we changed our minds about helping (or at least some of us) when previously we wouldn’t have taken time for “those people” it was because we had previously judged people based on our past experiences.

The crises forced us to deal with the present instead of the damaged neural pathways that are like a muddy rut of toxic waste.

Read on to learn more about the toxic waste and how it surfaces in icky ways.

DON'T GET SUCKED INTO THE MUDDY RUT OR YOU WILL GET BURIED UNDER THE TOXIC WASTE

THE BODY KEEPS THE SCORE

Dr. Bessel van der Kolk, one of the world's foremost experts on trauma, has spent over 30 years working with survivors of abuse. In his book *The Body Keeps the Score - Brain, Mind And Body In The Healing of Trauma*, he explores the fascinating ways trauma doesn't just affect your mind, but actually takes up residence in your body as well.

Thanks to recent scientific advances, we now better understand the incredible power of the mind and that it is neuralplastic and changeable. What we need to realize is that trauma is a fact of life and can literally rewire your brain and body in a negative direction, pushing things like joy, connection, self-control, and trust to the backburner or even burying them out of sight in the subconscious mind.

I mentioned how common trauma is and as we know, many veterans and their families live with the painful aftermath of combat. More shocking causes of Post Traumatic Stress Disorder (PTSD) is that one in five Americans has been sexually assaulted; one in four grew up with alcoholics; one in three couples has engaged in physical violence; and one in four students is bullied.

Consider police officers, firefighters, first responders, criminal justice workers, doctors, medical staff, counselors, social workers and now even teachers and legislators are facing violence and threats of violence. We are all at risk in one way or another.

Dr. Kolk has more than 50 pages of references to the research that has been done on trauma over the years and how it impacts the brain. He is joined by another psychiatrist and researcher Dr Anna Lembke who wrote the book *Dopamine Nation, Finding Balance in the Age of Indulgence* as they both address how we cope with trauma at times in destructive ways, both to ourselves and to others..

In both of their books they talk about "the pain of pleasure and the pleasure of pain." I know it's hard to comprehend that we would find pleasure in pain, but think about it for a moment...why, when we know we are going to be hungover the next day and feel awful after getting drunk, do we do it anyway?

Why, after eating that 3rd piece of pizza or having another donut or dish of ice cream do we wonder why we are overweight and feel poorly? Yet at the next opportunity we give in and do it again?

The same with any addictive habit...we love it, and then we hate it. We are best served when our brain chemistry is at what scientists call "homeostasis" when we are, as I visualize, being comfortable to just "stay at home" in our own reality. No anxiety, no depression, just feeling good doing whatever life brings us.

But when trauma, or anything else scary or uncomfortable happens, our fight or flight response kicks in and our brains become more like a windshield wiper. We go from the "ugh this feels bad! I need to fix this pain so I think I will have a couple of drinks" and the brainshield wiper is now on the pleasure side...at least for the moment.

The next thing we know is that the car is wrecked, the wallet is empty and the cops are on their way and you know you are not going to pass the test. You are now on the pain side again. What are you going to do now? That solution didn't work so well.

So the cop lets you go and you are happy but yet stressed out so what do you do? Go home and have a drink to calm down? Or celebrate?

Maybe the cycle is food, shopping, pornography or any other kind of "pleasure response," Too much of anything usually ends up in an unpleasant result that can be emotionally, physically or financially painful and may even cause another trauma (going to jail, having a partner leave you, a medical crises, bankruptcy, etc.).

This happens with our trauma responses as well. We think we have let go of things and then we have a trigger and we are right back there in painful memories.

There are therapeutic techniques that can be beneficial that do use revisiting the event, and I do use some of those, but I have found that talk therapy can, at times, keep people stuck for years in the hurt, anger, shame, guilt, ruminating and raging.

I have found a way that has brought complete healing to dozens of my clients who had Complex Post Traumatic Stress Disorder C-PTSD and were stuck. No matter which therapeutic tool is used, it requires a willingness to go through some pain to get to the other side, but it is worth it!

EASIER SAID THAN DONE

I am not intending to trivialize anyone's trauma and make it sound like you just ignore it or blow it off, or stuff it down like it never happened.

That is not what I am saying and as hard as it is, and as much as we may try to rationalize ruminating and talking about how poorly we have been treated, the point is, you get to decide if it is helpful for you to think about it on any given day. Not that you can prevent the memory from popping into your head, but you can choose to dismiss it...for the moment.

As a survivor of several traumatic events, I can tell you that those memories no longer make me sick. They are still there, but when there is a trigger and the pop up I take authority over them, because I am no longer a victim of trauma.

I am in charge of my thoughts and I get to decide if they will disrupt my serenity or if there is any reason I need to focus on them at this moment.

Yes I do still see a counselor for "a tune up" once in a while. I do have an AA sponsor, I have gone to Alanon, I do have a business coach and an amazing pastor and spiritual mentors over the years.

I also have a wonderful husband and friends who help me process past hurts, hangups and habits. I am here to tell you that letting go of trauma is possible.

My experience, and that of all my clients who have healed from trauma, will tell you that you can't and don't need to do it alone.

Even when a trigger brings something back, I now release it as something that happened. I ask God to help me make a willful decision to forgive that person or accept that situation as it is–a painful thing of the past that I can't do anything about that I will not let destroy me.

It may be forgiving myself for something I may have done, or not done, that contributed to my or someone else's trauma in some way.

I can choose to not give my mental and emotional energy to something I couldn't then, and still can't control, so why surrender my sanity now?

This is a mindful decision that takes practice. Once you become aware that an uncomfortable thought has popped up, you can ask yourself, "Is this a helpful thought? Do I need to keep it?" If not, you can reject it before it is replanted into your memory.

Sometimes it's not a major traumatic event. It might be an irritating politician, a nosy neighbor, an obnoxious relative, or a difficult coworker who stirs up frustration and creates a toxic cocktail in your brain.

These are the things that keep us focused on the negative and unwillingness to collaborate with people that are different from us.

No wonder so many of us feel like a mess. Isn't it time to change your mind and clean up your brain? If you haven't yet learned how to manage these toxic thoughts, you're likely to end up in an even worse mental state than you were in right after the trauma.

Just as a muddy road can't pull you back into its ruts once you stop driving down it, our minds can be rewired through consistent, positive focus. You can not only reject that negative thought, but you can quickly choose to create a new neural pathway by a new script.

But how? By intentionally practicing the positivity of the 3 G's, we create new neural pathways that resist keeping us stuck and once you start living in a positive mindset you can get as addicted to being positive as you have been to being negative. It's up to you.

EMOTIONAL FREEDOM – A TECHNIQUE TO TAP YOUR WAY TO PEACE

There are many ways that mental health practitioners use our bodies to reprogram our brains. EMDR (Eye Movement Desensitization and Reprocessing) is a light therapy that uses rapid movement of the eyes as you are looking at rapidly moving lights to help heal traumatic memories.

My friend and colleague Dr. Dave Macintyre told me about Brain Spotting, a technique he uses and trains others to use, that has helped many of the clients he has worked with. The technique was developed by Dr. David Grand and it works by pairing a client's steady focus on an external spot with body sensations so the nervous system can release what's been trapped

I am not going to go into those here but I do want to share a technique that I use often that has been a great help to every client that I have used it with. It is called Emotional Freedom Technique (EFT) Tapping and the foundation was developed by Dr. Roger Callahan, a clinical psychologist discovered in the 1980s, that tapping on specific acupressure points could rapidly alleviate his client's phobias and emotional distress.

In the early 1990s Gary Craig, a Stanford-educated engineer, simplified the method and developed the Emotional Freedom Technique EFT that is more of a one size fit's all model. I do a modified version that is really helpful.It is a remarkable way of telling your nervous system, "Hey, we are safe! We are capable. We can handle this. We can turn off the emergency alarm and tapping helps shift your brain out of panic mode.

I have a couple videos on my YouTube channel to show you how to do this and one is made for kids, but there are tons of people who teach this. I just add a couple other things to it that I have been told by my clients and students make it a great experience.

On the next page there is a diagram of where to tap and then I include a simple script of what you could say to yourself if you have had something bad happen that you are struggling with. Some of my clients have found tapping the tips of their fingers together or on the table or desk really helps and is a discreet way to deal with stress at work or school though it's not a specific acupressure point.

MERIDIAN POINTS TO TAP ON

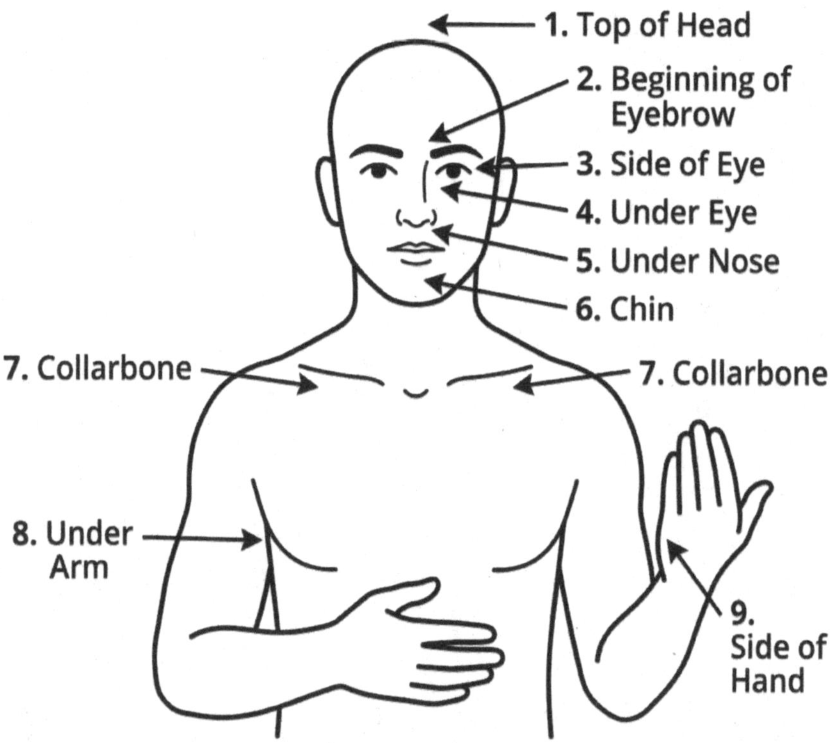

Here is the tapping sequence to use and the script to go through. After this, from now on, no matter what your situation, you can write your own script for it. This works great with kids too, especially those on the autism spectrum.

First think about where your stress level is when you think about a stressful event. Let's use having to give a speech or a report in front of a large room of people as an example. Give it a number from 1-10 with 10 being super stressed. Now, follow the script as you start tapping.

Tap gently on each point about 10 times. It is okay if you feel scared. It is part of the process.

- Top of head: It is scary to be in front of people. I am afraid I will mess up.
- Beginning of eyebrow: I have been made fun of in the past and it hurt.
- Side of eye: They laughed and I was embarrassed.
- Under eye: It made me sick to my stomach and I felt bad all night.
- Under nose: I couldn't quit thinking about it.
- Chin: It isn't my fault that these memories distress me.
- Collarbone: But today I am going to release the tension in my body.
- Under arm: I will give myself permission to heal.

THE REPROGRAMING

Repeat the cycle once more, but shift the focus:

- Top of head: I am more than what happened to me.
- Beginning of eyebrow: I am capable and I can do a great job
- Side of eye: I am grateful for my strength.
- Under eye: I am good at letting go of the pain and shame.
- Under nose: I am smart and resilient and I will do a great speech
- Chin: I will be proud of myself for doing my best
- Collarbone: I will not let anyone take away my confidence because I am safe in my own skin and life today.

- Under arm: I am walking toward a new future and leaving the old one behind.

A PEACEFUL REFLECTION

With hands over your heart, breathe in, hold it while you say "I am courageous to face this. I am gentle with myself. I will walk proudly and do my best. It's ok if people don't like me. Blow out as long as you can. Keep up the breath work 4 times saying – I breathe in peace, and blow out stress… breathe in confidence, blow out fear etc.

GO TO YOUR SAFE PLACE

Imagine the most beautiful place you have ever been. Look around, take in the colors, the beauty, the peace. Take a deep breath, smell the air and feel the comfort against your skin. Now rest there. Feel the love of your creator and the peace of letting go of your pain. You are free here and you can come to this safe place anytime to leave the pain of a bad memory. You are a victor here. Bask in it.

Now take an inventory of what number you are at…is your stress lower? That is the goal!

So the next time a toxic thought arises, pause and decide: Which road do you want to travel—the muddy, deeply rutted one that keeps you stuck, or the new one that is smooth, straight, and leading you somewhere better?

THE HARD WAY
THE GOOD WAY
ROTTEN POTATOES
BAD MEMORIES
BAD MEMORIES
ANGER
VIOLENCE
DIRT
ROTTEN POTATOES
GREAT JOB
I DID IT
BEAUTIFUL VIEW
WONDERFUL SMELL
FEELS SMOOTH
SOUNDS COMFORTING
FAMILY
FRIENDS
HOME

RESCUE STORY #4 – TAMMY – THE ALCOHOLIC SOCIAL WORKER

I first met Tammy when she applied to volunteer to be on our Board of Directors at Randlin Homes, our non-profit organization for homeless veterans and other adults who were struggling with mental health and addictions.

Tammy understood alcoholism and mental health issues. She had her bachelor's degree in Psychology and had been working in the field for a while. Personally, she struggled with alcoholism induced by trauma that she did not deal with from 9 years ago.

She actually died from her own alcohol abuse and fortunately was brought back to life and decided to remain sober and vowed to help other people in recovery as a way to show gratitude for her new life.

By the time she came to us she had already been sober for a couple of years, but she was still struggling with what led up to her becoming sober and how to cope with the memories of it all.

You see in the throes of her alcoholism, Tammy's mom died in a tragic house fire and she was very angry about it. Tammy's relationship with her mom was less than healthy as it is in most families where addiction is active and she didn't know how to reconcile all the feelings around it.

She also blamed herself for not being able to get her mom out of the house during the fire. She tried to live with the feelings of hating herself, guilt, shame...what do you do with it all? She chose to try to drink herself to death.

Tammy was an amazing board member and proved herself to be an irreplaceable asset to the organization so we hired her to be the house manager. She was amazing with the residents and became a champion of the 3 G's using them every day to help them start to improve their thinking.

It didn't take long for her to help them recognize how much they had to be grateful for, how to improve their self-esteem by realizing all the things they were good at and improve their life by reaching the goals they set every day.

Tammy was also a reporter for our local newspaper and helped edit my second book, "Speak to Me God I'm Listening-365 Daily Meditations for Those Who Want to Hear God Answer Life's Toughest Questions" and now she has helped with this book as well.

Tammy has made evident the power of the 3 G's by the successes she had with the dozens of residents she has worked with since we started using the 3 G's. She also started doing the 3 G's religiously and has transformed her own life by dealing with her trauma and she just celebrated 15 years of sobriety.

FOOD FOR THOUGHT SECTION:

1. What traumatic things have you been through that you are still dwelling on? Abuse? Accident? Death of a loved one? Divorce? Bullying?

2. How has this trauma impacted your physical, emotional, social and spiritual well being?

3. What negative thoughts or behaviors come to mind that you need to release?

4. Who do you need to reach out to that can help you on your journey?

JOURNALING THE 3 G'S AND MORE

CHAPTER 5:

THE MIND-BODY-SPIRIT CONNECTION

SPIRITUAL AWAKENING AND WHY IT HELPS

Like I have said before, If it wasn't for discovering that the Bible had some really good sound advice and the hope for a new life, I wouldn't even be here and certainly wouldn't be writing another book about it.

Some of you may be going, "UGH- I don't believe the Bible and don't want to hear it."

Some may be saying, "Why would I want to believe it? Christians are just hypocrites."

Others may be wondering, "How is it connected to reprogramming the brain?

What I want to do is to share with you the things that have helped me, many of my client's, my family, and a boatload of other people that God has led me to cross paths with, who are better because I have 50 years of testing this "God thing" and "Bible stuff" and have found solutions that I could not find anywhere else.

In fact, if you get even one thing out of this book that you can use in a positive way, then you can at least believe that it was a good thing that Jesus lived and that we have the Bible, because that is why I am here today.

CRISES PRAYERS, TOUGH QUESTIONS AND NEUROLOGICAL BENEFITS OF PRAYER

Some people say they don't believe in God or a higher power but have you ever been in a crisis with a sick child, a car accident, a near death experience? Perhaps you have watched storm chasers or people caught live on camera after a tornado.

What are people doing in what they may think could be their last moments during one of those scary situations? Most of them that I have seen are praying, "God help me."

They may not have any idea who they are praying to, but it gives people a sense of not being alone, and hope for either getting through the situation alive or having a place to go to that is not a horrible place if they die.

I found an interesting article in the Library of Science called "The convergent neuroscience of Christian prayer and attachment relationships in the context of mental health: a systematic review." that offers some food for thought.

In short, they found that prayer activates some of the same brain systems that are involved when we form close, emotional bonds with other people. In particular, it lights up areas linked to the brain's "default mode network" and "theory of mind" — regions we use to understand other people's thoughts and feelings and to relate socially.

In other words, praying makes us feel good and helps our mental health. I actually had a client just today who said "I have been praying like crazy to get through things and I feel peace. It's really weird," he said. "I don't understand it but it feels good."

Faith is believing in the unseen, and since I can't see heaven, or God, or Jesus, I have simply made a choice to believe.

And as far as the Bible goes; it is confusing and at times upsetting but I choose to find what makes sense to me and use it for the good because it helps me, and it gives me hope.

To be perfectly transparent, that means that I don't spend a ton of time on a lot of the Old Testament because all those rules and regulations make no sense to me but then I guess they don't need to.

Like I don't need to understand why God made us with this elimination process that results in the need for toilet paper. It's like, come on God… couldn't you have come up with a less complicated and gross process? God does not get mad when we ask Him tough questions so go ahead. (He hasn't answered me on that one yet!)

Unfortunately, many Christians over the years have used the Bible as a battering ram to beat people into submission rather than what it was written for which is to bring people to a loving God.

If you have missed out on the encouragement you could be getting from these words of wisdom because all you have heard is "shame on you," that is heartbreaking, and I am genuinely sorry.

I hope you can, at minimum, be open to considering that the Bible offers some really good life tips that are just as good as Confucius or Buddha or Mohammad or Maya Angelou or Tony Robbins or Mel Robbins or even Bill W.

BILL W. AND SPIRITUAL AWAKENINGS

Who is Bill W. you ask? Anyone who has ever gone to Alcoholics Anonymous (AA) would know that he, along with Dr. Bob was one of the co-founders of AA. When they wrote the 12 steps they used the "God as we understand Him" concept to encourage people in their recovery. But how did they get started?

Well, before their meeting, Bill and Dr. Bob had each been in contact with the Oxford Group which was a Christian organization founded by American Lutheran minister Frank Buchman in 1921 who shared with them what had been working with the men who had gotten sober in the Oxford Group.

Originally, the Oxford Group was under the name "First Century Christian Fellowship." Buchman believed that fear and selfishness were the root of all problems. He also believed that the solution to living without fear and selfishness was to "surrender one's life over to God's plan".

The Oxford Group's recovery program featured a "surrender to Jesus Christ by sharing with others how lives had been changed in the pursuit of four moral absolutes: honesty, purity, unselfishness, and love."

This non-alcoholic fellowship emphasized universal spiritual values in daily living. The Episcopal clergyman, Dr. Samuel Shoemaker, led the Oxford Groups in the U.S. and eventually Bill W and Dr. Bob decided to take the concept to a broader view to include a "higher power" for those who may be atheist or agnostic or a part of some other religious belief system.

I did not go to my first AA meeting until March of 1996. I knew nothing about the 12 steps. When I compare my own journey that started 20 years before that, I got sober using Bible verses. They are very comparable to these steps and I like the structure and process of healing that the 12 steps bring.

In addition, since going to graduate school and learning about Cognitive Behavioral Therapy (CBT), Neurolinguistic Programming (NLP), Dialectical Behavioral Therapy (DBT) and so many other therapeutic approaches to recovery, I have found that these foundational belief systems were scientifically and medically validated and consistent with Biblical teachings.

Check the following out to see what you think.

WISDOM FROM THE "GOOD BOOK"

Like I said AA's foundation was from a Christian perspective. Since then there are an estimated 30-50 different 12 step groups that have used these ideas for recovery of a wide variety of things. Here are just a few..

- COSLAA – CoSex and Love Addicts Anonymous, for friends and family of people with a sex or love addiction, associated with SLAA

- DA – Debtors Anonymous
- EA – Emotions Anonymous, for recovery from mental and emotional illness
- FA – Families Anonymous, for relatives and friends of addicts
- FA – Food Addicts in Recovery Anonymous
- FAA – Food Addicts Anonymous
- GA – Gamblers Anonymous
- Gam-Anon and Gam-A-Teen, for friends and family members of problem gamblers
- HA – Heroin Anonymous
- MA – Marijuana Anonymous
- NA – Narcotics Anonymous
- N/A – Neurotics Anonymous, for recovery from mental and emotional illness
- Nar-Anon, for friends and family members of addicts
- NicA – Nicotine Anonymous
- OA – Overeaters Anonymous
- PA – Pills Anonymous, for recovery from prescription pill addiction
- RA – Racists Anonymous
- R-A- Recoveries Anonymous
- SA – Sexaholics Anonymous
- SAA – Sex Addicts Anonymous
- SCA – Sexual Compulsives Anonymous
- SIA – Survivors of Incest Anonymous
- SLAA – Sex and Love Addicts Anonymous
- SRA – Sexual Recovery Anonymous
- UA – Underearners Anonymous
- WA – Workaholics Anonymous

In addition there are lots of Christian 12 step programs now too like Celebrate Recovery, Life Recovery, and others that use the Bible comparisons to the 12 Steps. To avoid any copyright infringements our organization Purpose Driven Recovery Academy, came up with our own version that uses some different scriptures and a wording that feels congruent to our mission.

1. We recognized we couldn't manage our addiction on our own and admitted that our lives were out of control and we couldn't handle them on our own.
   "For I have the desire to do what is right, but not the ability to carry it out." (Romans 7:18)

2. We chose to trust God's power to restore our minds and hearts.
   "For it is God who works in you, both to will and to work for his good pleasure." (Philippians 2:13)

3. We surrendered our will to God, asking Him to lead our lives.
   "Trust in the Lord with all your heart, and do not lean on your own understanding. In all your ways acknowledge him, and he will make straight your paths." (Proverbs 3:5-6)

4. We took an honest inventory—looking courageously at patterns, choices, and consequences.
   "Let us test and examine our ways, and return to the Lord!" (Lamentations 3:40)

5. We acknowledged and shared the true nature of our wrongs—to God, to ourselves, and to a trusted person.
   "Therefore, confess your sins to one another and pray for one another, that you may be healed." (James 5:16)

6. We became willing to let God reshape us, including the character flaws driving the behavior. "Humble yourselves before the Lord, and he will exalt you." (James 4:10)

7. We asked God to remove what harms us, one step at a time.
   "If we confess our sins, he is faithful and just to forgive us our sins and to cleanse us from all unrighteousness." (1 John 1:9)

8. We identified who we have hurt and developed the willingness to make things right.

"And as you wish that others would do to you, do so to them." (Luke 6:31)

9. We made amends where possible, while choosing safety and wisdom, so repair doesn't create more harm to others.
   "So if you are offering your gift at the altar and there remember that your brother has something against you, leave your gift there before the altar and go. First be reconciled to your brother, and then come and offer your gift." (Matthew 5:23–24)

10. We kept checking our hearts and behavior, and when we were wrong, we corrected it quickly.
    "Search me, O God, and know my heart! Try me and know my thoughts! And see if there be any grievous way in me, and lead me in the way everlasting!" (Psalm 139-23-24)

11. We strengthened our relationship with God through prayer and reflection, asking for His guidance and the power to follow His will for us. "Do not be conformed to this world, but be transformed by the renewal of your mind, that by testing you may discern what is the will of God, what is good and acceptable and perfect." (Romans 12:2)

12. As God changed us, we tried to live it out and encourage others, applying these principles in daily life.
    "Blessed be the God and Father of our Lord Jesus Christ, the Father of mercies and God of all comfort, who comforts us in all our affliction, so that we may be able to comfort those who are in any affliction, with the comfort with which we ourselves are comforted by God." (2 Corinthians 1:3-4)

GOOD BOOK

GOOD MESSAGE

GOOD THOUGHTS

GOOD BEHAVIORS

STEP 11 AND 12

Looking at the 12 step program it sure seems to fit with the process of the 3 G's and reprogramming your brain.

Step 11 talks about "praying and reflecting/meditating and having conscious contact with God." This is the time when you think about what you are Grateful for.

During those first moments of the day as you are doing that you also "pray for knowing what His will is for you." This is where you ask Him to tell you what he has gifted you with that you are Good at that he will then direct you to do which is His will and your Goals for the day.

I listen to a YouTube channel called Grace Prayer that you can find at https://www.youtube.com/@GracePrayer-s that reminds me every morning to start my day with seeking God's will and not getting all wound up about my day before it even starts.

On that channel, James shares verses like I am going to, that show the biblical support for a healthy mind and body by taking control of our thoughts, and having that "conscious contact" with God. He talks about changing our neural pathways and I have never had a client who has listened to a message I send them that hasn't found great comfort that always seems to be just what they need to hear when they need to hear it.

Because habits are hard for me (hence a book I am writing on habits from personal experience,) my husband bought me a book called the Weekly Habits Project- a Challenge to Journal, Reflect and Make Tiny Changes for Big Results put out by Zondervan Press that helps you get to the bottom of why you aren't sticking to your habits.

I am on week 2 called "Our Minds" and it challenges you to think about what you think about that keeps you from getting quiet and doing your 3 G's and other habits. The end result of my meditation and journaling time today came up with an acronym- PAWALAD

Because I have ADHD I need tricks to help me remember and it is easier to trigger my memory with an acronym so PAWALAD means

Pray And Wait And Listen And Do. Praying is great but if you don't listen to what God is saying to you then you won't know what He wants you to do next.

One of my favorite verses to support this is Joshua 1:8 where he writes "[8] Keep this Book of the Law always on your lips; meditate on it day and night, so that you may be careful to do everything written in it. Then you will be prosperous and successful."

This is the basis of the 3G's method. Though my book is not a law, what I am sharing, including these Bible verses are great tools and if you can follow the things you learn here and "meditate on them day and night" you can't fail because when your mind will be on gratitude it can't be on being angry at the same time. It's impossible.

Let's look at a few more words of wisdom from "The Good Book."

PAWALAD
Pray And Wait
And Listen And Do

HUMOR AND WISDOM IN THE BIBLE FROM A WISE DUMB MAN

The book of Solomon is often referred to as "the book of wisdom." Solomon was the King who wrote it and he was basically the biblical poster child for "How to be incredibly wise and still do really dumb things."

Solomon started out great. He loved God, asked for wisdom instead of money or fame, and God was so pleased He gave him all three.

Solomon wrote Proverbs, settled disputes with supernatural insight, and became famous for his wisdom. If anyone looked like "God's golden boy," it was Solomon.

And then... he discovered women. Lots of them.

Even though God clearly warned Israel's kings not to collect horses, gold, and wives like trophies—and especially not to marry women who worshiped other gods—Solomon did all three.

He married 700 foreign wives, collected 300 concubines, and built temples for their idols. It was like he read God's "Do Not Do" list and treated it as a bucket list.

So how could he still be God's chosen king and a wise man? Because God's calling and gifts don't automatically disappear the moment we start acting foolish. Our Good at list remains things we are good at...unfortunately, sometimes we get good at doing self-destructive bad things.

Solomon was genuinely gifted with wisdom, genuinely chosen, and genuinely used by God—and he was also genuinely stubborn, distracted, and disobedient. He shows us that you can be wise in your head and still be a mess in your habits and your heart.

In the end, Solomon's story is both comforting and sobering:

- Comforting, because it proves God can still work through very imperfect people.

- Sobering, because even the wisest person on earth can ruin their legacy if they stop listening to the God who gave them that wisdom in the first place.

In other words: you can be smart, called, and anointed—and still blow it if you think you're the exception to God's boundaries. Solomon was brilliant, but he wasn't the exception. Neither are we.

Why did Solomon do these things? In his mind they were logical ways to grow his kingdom and wealth but like many of our leaders (and all of us to be honest) we make all kinds of compromises to get rich or meet our own selfish needs.

Solomon was no different. He, along with other nations were trying to get along and form alliances so they used/traded women, along with other things to make deals.

The 700 royal wives were from the bloodlines of other royal leaders and the concubines were women from other nations who were brought into his household to strengthen ties between kingdoms.

Concubines lived with a man and had a sexual relationship with him, had a lower social status than a wife and often did not have the full legal rights, protections, or inheritance status that a wife and her children had.

Here's what I think about that setup... I think some of these women were not happy campers and with 1000 of them it will be no surprise that Solomon had some challenges within his household and shared these words of wisdom he learned from when you don't follow what God says to begin with.

Proverbs 21:19 "It is better to live in a desert land than with a quarrelsome and fretful woman."

It may appear Solomon is repeating himself because he says the same thing 4 chapters later, but don't assume he is talking about the same wife. Remember he had 1000 wives and I expect many of them felt left out, taken advantage of and used and perhaps didn't hesitate to share their thoughts about the whole thing.

Here are just a few of the 915 verses in the book of Proverbs that tell me that Solomon learned some hard things over the years living life as he did.

Proverbs 25:24 "It is better to live in a corner of the housetop than in a house shared with a quarrelsome wife."

Proverbs 27:15-16 "A continual dripping on a rainy day and a quarrelsome wife are alike; to restrain her is to restrain the wind or to grasp oil in one's right hand."

Proverbs 11:22 "Like a gold ring in a pig's spout is a beautiful woman without discretion."

Proverbs 6:27-29 "Can a man carry fire next to his chest and his clothes not be burned? Or can one walk on hot coals and his feet not be scorched? So is he who goes into his neighbor's wife; none who touches her will go unpunished."

Proverbs 6:32-33 "He who commits adultery lacks sense; he who does it destroys himself. He will get wounds and dishonor, and his disgrace will not be wiped away."

Proverbs 20:1 "Wine is a mocker, strong drink is raging: and whosoever is deceived thereby is not wise."

Proverbs 23:20-21 "Be not among drunkards or among gluttonous eaters of meat for the drunkard and the glutton will come to poverty and slumber will clothe them with rags."

Proverbs 23:26-28 "My son, give me your heart, and let your eyes observe my ways. For a prostitute is a deep pit; an adulteress is a narrow well. She lies in wait like a robber and increases the traitors among mankind."

Proverbs 23:29-30 "Who has woe? Who has sorrow? Who has contentions? Who has babbling? Who has wounds without cause? Who has redness of eyes? They that tarry long at the wine; they that go to seek mixed wine."

Proverbs 15:1 “A soft answer turns away wrath, but a harsh word stirs up anger.”

Proverbs 15:18 “A hot-tempered person stirs up conflict, but the one who is patient calms a quarrel.”

Proverbs 29:11 “Fools give full vent to their rage, but the wise bring calm in the end.”

Proverbs 21:29 “The wicked put up a bold front, but the upright give thought to their ways.”

Proverbs 11:25 “Whoever brings blessing will be enriched, and one who waters will himself be watered.”

Proverbs 4:26-27 “Give careful thought to the paths for your feet and be steadfast in all your ways. Do not turn to the right or the left; keep your foot from evil.”

So there you have it... just a few things to add to your “What Would Linda Say” list but consider this; on that last verse, notice it says “give careful thought.”

Our thoughts are what gets it all going and if we don’t want to get sick from toxic thoughts, we need to actually think about what thoughts we have floating through our minds and ask ourselves if they are helpful or not. We need to choose to not walk down that path of destruction.

The secret is to be mindful and manage everything that goes into your mind. For example, if someone calls you stupid or ugly, most of us automatically put that in our memory banks and ruminate on it, sometimes for the rest of our lives.

Come on now, you know it’s true! You still have feelings rising up about that kid that made fun of you, or something someone said that got you all riled up don’t you? If not, AWESOME!

The fact is, studies show that we really can’t multi-task like we think we can and if your MIND is FULL (mindful) of positive thoughts, there is no room for the negative. If your mind is on all this good advice you won’t go down the wrong road.

My encouragement: you don't have to accept every hurtful word that comes your way.

Instead, pause and examine it. Ask yourself if there is any good reason to store that comment or experience in your memory and let it take up space in your heart and body. Is it really worth holding on to something that will only make you feel worse?

Decide, right then and there, to let it go. Reject it. Don't get sucked into the muddy rut where all of those other negative memories have gone that eventually sit in your subconscious mind, wreaking havoc.

BE MINDFUL OF EVERY THOUGHT BECAUSE WHEN YOUR MIND IS FULL OF POSITIVES YOU CAN'T BE NEGATIVE AT THE SAME TIME

WHY IS THIS SO HARD?

This may seem like a bit of a dichotomy but that is kind of what we talked about with the pain/pleasure thing, and if you are going to roll with some of this Bible stuff, here is a possible explanation that will give you food for thought about spiritual forces.

The Bible talks about us being "double-minded." God did not make puppets. He doesn't force anyone to do anything. He could, but he doesn't.

So the mess our world, our bodies, our finances, our relationships and much more are in, has largely come about because of our own choices. OUCH! But let's be honest, we are tempted to get that quick fix, and there it is, that pain/pleasure response again.

We want fast and more money, so we modify foods to produce more, faster, and then we add addictive products like sugar, alcohol, THC and only God knows what other kinds of toxic products that destroy us in countless ways, just so we (as fallible humans) can get what we want faster and better. Come on now, be honest. Do you see my point?

The Apostle Paul (previously known as Saul) knew all about this, and he learned the hard way. He had been a religious leader who was known to be the most relentless persecutor of Christians, even ordering them to be put to death because they followed Jesus.

Paul loved the power of being in charge, judging, and punishing people for not doing what he thought they should be doing, but God had a better plan for him, and like Solomon and many others, He had a lesson for him.

After Jesus died, Saul was on his way to Damascus when he saw a bright light and heard a voice say "Saul, Saul, why do you persecute me?" It was Jesus, and the next thing he knew, BAM, Saul was blinder than a bat (minus the super hearing power bats have) and having to be led to town, where Jesus said he would give him further instructions.

When Paul got to Damascus, a man named Ananias came looking for him after God had told Ananias to go heal this killer that everyone was afraid of. He is not excited about it, but he did it anyway.

Paul realized after having been totally blind for 3 days, fasting, and praying to be healed and then having some guy show up and lay hands on him and heal him, that maybe it was time to go down a different path because the one he had been on was not sparking joy anymore.

Jesus changed Saul's name to Paul and sent him on his way to start sharing the gospel.

After Paul had been in ministry for a while, he realized it was really hard to do the right thing all the time. He had been an arrogant, judgmental, angry guy, and those habits are hard to break, and he wrote about it in the book of Romans and I love Paul's honest admission of what a mess he was when he admitted that he didn't have it all together,

In Romans chapter 7 he helps those of us who need repetition to get things through our thick skulls by repeating himself. It also helps that he is an important leader and still screws up like the rest of us.

Here are verses 15-25 from Romans chapter 7 broken up a little so I don't break my rule of short paragraphs.

15 For I do not understand my own actions. For I do not do what I want, but I do the very thing I hate. 16 Now if I do what I do not want, I agree with the law, that it is good. 17 So now it is no longer I who do it, but sin that dwells within me.

18 For I know that nothing good dwells in me, that is, in my flesh. For I have the desire to do what is right, but not the ability to carry it out. 19 For I do not do the good I want, but the evil I do not want is what I keep on doing. 20 Now if I do what I do not want, it is no longer I who do it, but sin that dwells within me.

21 So I find it to be a law that when I want to do right, evil lies close at hand. 22 For I delight in the law of God, in my inner being, 23 but I see in my members another law waging war against the law of my mind and making me captive to the law of sin that dwells in my members.

24 Wretched man that I am! Who will deliver me from this body of death? 25 Thanks be to God through Jesus Christ our Lord! So then, I myself serve the law of God with my mind, but with my flesh I serve the law of sin."

What does that mean "the devil made me do it?" What Paul is saying is that we are born with a predisposition to get our needs met. This is a good thing. It is our autonomic nervous system doing the self-protection thing that keeps us alive.

But we also observe the world around us and learn unhealthy, hurtful ways of getting what we perceive to be a need when in reality, it is just a selfish want. How much of this is learned and how much is already inside of us is not really clear.

For example, babies cry when they are hungry or in pain. We get an adrenal rush when we realize that a bear is chasing and this superpower helps us run fast and far. These are good things but somewhere along the line, we get selfish.

If you are a parent, think back to that first time your child said "no" or threw a dish at you because they didn't want to eat those peas. Or remember that first time they whacked a sibling, saying "mine" when they were asked to share.

My daughter bit another child in Sunday school when she was about two years old. She was upset because the little girl wouldn't share and I promise you I never taught her how to bite anyone to get her way!

All the way back to the Garden of Eden, the devil is tempting Adam and Eve, suggesting that God wasn't playing fair by not giving them more than what they had when, in fact, they had everything they could possibly need in Eden.

But no...like us...Adam and Eve were not satisfied with what they had. Always wanting more, more, more. We have to keep trying to get comfortable being uncomfortable.

PETER COULD RELATE

Peter had the same problem. Now here is a guy who was so dedicated to Jesus that he didn't want the Romans to arrest Jesus, so he grabbed his sword and whacked off the ear of one of the Roman guards, which, of course, Jesus had to miraculously fix since that was not the way Jesus did things.

Jesus demonstrated when he told Peter that God saw Peter's strong faith and that He would be the rock of the church. Jesus told Him that, for God's will to be performed, He must die. Then what does Peter say?

Matthew 16:22-23 says "And Peter took him aside and began to rebuke him, saying, "Far be it from you, Lord This shall never happen to you."

Jesus turned and said to Peter, "Get behind me, Satan! You are a hindrance to me. For you are not setting your mind on the things of God, but on the things of man."

What was Jesus saying here? Peter wasn't Satan, but he certainly was being influenced to do what the devil would have liked, which was to end the ministry Jesus had on earth, so Jesus told Peter was wrong? It was where his mind was focused so he needed to change his thinking.

My mom used to say, "There is an angel on one shoulder and a devil on the other so be careful which one you listen to."

And therein lies the root of all our problems. We are torn between the good and the bad, the positive and the negative, the couch and the gym. We want what we want when we want it.

James 4:17 says, "So whoever knows the right thing to do and fails to do it, for him it is sin," and Romans 6:23 says "For the wages of sin is death, but the free gift of God is eternal life in Christ Jesus our Lord."

Don't look at those verses as dogmatic, guilt-tripping, shaming statements. Look at them from a scientific standpoint and replace the word "sin" with not doing what will keep us healthy.

WE DON'T JUST DIE- WE KILL OURSELVES

The very first line in the first lesson of my Physical Education course video from the University of Wisconsin Superior when I was in undergraduate school, was "we don't just die, we kill ourselves."

It went on to talk about us not doing what we know we should be doing by eating healthy, staying hydrated with water, (not alcohol, coffee and energy drinks,) exercise (which includes more than getting up from the couch and walking to the refrigerator) and sleep (at least 7-8 hours a night.)

The fact is, we all die but we will die much sooner if we are doing some of the things we learned about in Proverbs. Things like overeating, smoking, doing drugs, drinking, not exercising, etc. There is a price to pay.

Of course we know that all kinds of studies show how what we eat impacts our bodies. As I touched on before the United States residents are overweight. In fact the US ranks in the top 15 fattest countries in the world averaging #10 in obesity rates.

Another shocking statistic is that 51% of people 12 and over have used illicit drugs, 1 in 10 people in the US 12 and over have an Alcohol Use Disorder! You read that right, 12 and older because the young people are looking at us adults and thinking that alcohol is a great way to cope.

So how do we make changes? How do we get to the point where we can change the perceived need to escape whatever feelings we have that are just too hard to deal with?

It is obvious that we think we need to cover up our bad feelings with something that can become so addictive that we are now "DIS-ORDERED" (hence the term substance abuse disorder, mental health disorder etc.)

If you haven't seen the movie "War Room" it is worth watching. I love how the main character fights the spiritual battle of her anger toward her husband by saying a similar thing to the song by Hillside- "Let the Devil Know Not Today."

I even had one of my clients who didn't even believe in God, or the devil, and she was walking around at work trying not to be annoyed at her coworker as she was saying to herself "not today, devil, not today!"

She was "taking every thought captive" like it talks about in II Corinthians 10:5, realizing that those negative, toxic thoughts did not have to enter her mind.

I have started working much more with female veterans suffering from MST known as Military Sexual Trauma. It was shocking to me to learn that some studies show that over 70% of women who have been in the military have been sexually assaulted or traumatized which often leads to other disorders including addictions.

Fortunately there is healing from even the worst kind of trauma. My following rescue story was one of those women who unfortunately departed this world last September after a long illness but she left a hero mark on the world despite her traumatic life experiences.

NOT TODAY,
DEVIL.

RESCUE STORY #5 – BECKY – THE VIETNAM VETERAN CARE PROVIDER WITH PTSD/MST

I met Becky at the Salvation Army homeless shelter, where she had been living since losing her job, her home, and everything in it because her PTSD had led her down a very dark path that she was stuck in.

Frankly, I didn't know, or couldn't remember much about what she actually did in the Navy, but I had helped her get her service connected disability because she had been sexually assaulted during her service time and it was really impacting her.

Becky passed away last September and since her family was not from Wisconsin, I arranged to bring her ashes to North Carolina. It wasn't until I contacted VFW Post 5352 to do a memorial service for her family that I got the details on what Becky did in the Navy during the Vietnam era..

Quartermaster Brian W. Bauer from the VFW put on an amazing ceremony and many of the veterans, none who ever knew Becky, showed up to offer their respects for their fellow veteran and hear just what a legacy she was leaving.

You see Brian was also in the Navy, many years after Becky but he researched her background and he told us that Becky was one of the first women in the United States military to serve in what they call combat roles.

When she began her service she was "non-rated, non-designated" with no MOS (which means Military Occupational Specialty.) She eventually was given the same designation as Brian, a Quartermaster who are petty officers involved with all things related to navigation of military vessels.

Eventually she was stationed in Puerto Rico and was assigned to port services as a line handler. Brian was amazed to discover that she would have been the person that would tie up and secure the tugs that would take out the submarine that he would have been on, in the very same port in Puerto Rico.

Becky seemed to be coping well when she got out. She found a job as a care provider at the VA but eventually her mental health deteriorated, her memories of the sexual assault that she had experienced while in the service, and many other things, led her to a state of hopelessness. She had no idea how she was going to recover.

Becky had relatives in the Wausau area and found shelter and the Salvation Army. Knowing that Ralph and I operated a program for homeless veterans they called me and told me they had a female veteran that needed help.

It was like God had brought me an angel to do what I could not do for all of the people in our program. We were growing rapidly and I was working full time and we now had a 4 bedroom group home and 4 apartments that had veterans who needed medication management and other help. More than we could give.

Becky gladly accepted the opportunity to move into one of our apartments, where she became the house mom to the men who lived there. One of those men was Chris, the heart patient who was one of our other rescue stories.

Becky became very Grateful, not only for shelter but for being able to rediscover what she was Good at. She now had Goals to provide service however she could and eventually get out on her own again.

As our residents got well enough to move to their own apartments, Becky became the person to get donations to support all their needs. Before long we had so many donations that we started a thrift store, which eventually led to being the primary support for housing, clothing, and food for our residents.

The organization exploded! We bought a 20 bed home and then a 7 bed home that Becky moved into and operated. There were many ups and downs but after several years, Becky eventually got her disability, bought her own personal home and moved several of the veterans into her own home.

I nominated Becky for the Red Cross Hometown Caregiver Hero of the year, which she received at a community-wide dinner in 2008, where she was shown much appreciation for her contribution to those who were not being served by the VA.

Becky used the three G's with her residents as well as the rest of the agency to encourage them to keep the faith, stay positive, be grateful, and never give up on their goals.

Like all of us she had her challenges. Mental illness does that to us and our friends and families, but she left a legacy of life and hope for many of the residents whose lives she touched.

Her message would be to never give up trying and never lose hope . The 3G's can help you do those things if you use them.

NEVER GIVE UP

NEVER LOSE HOPE

GOD HAS A PURPOSE

FOR YOU

WHAT IS YOUR MINDSET? THINK ON THESE THINGS

If this is your first taste of seriously considering the value of the Bible, I hope you're starting to see that there's actually some really good—and very practical—wisdom in there.

If you want to find verses on how to change your mind (or just make sure you're not losing it!), you can go to https://www.openbible.info/topics/ and type in any topic you're curious about. It's kind of like "Google for Bible verses," without having to wade through 47,000 random opinions first.

I would, however, encourage you to always pay attention to the context of the verses you find, or things can get a little confusing—or even downright weird. The Bible isn't a Magic 8-Ball or a spiritual fortune cookie. You can't just shake it, pull out one line, and build your whole life on it.

So read around the verse, or the whole chapter and see who's talking, who they're talking to, and what's going on. That's where it really starts to come alive.

The book of Philippians, Chapter 4 is my main go-to, which is really the foundation of the 3G's and if we were to commit to doing this throughout the day, every day, we would not have to worry about the bag of rotten potatoes or the muddy ruts!

Paul wrote this book to the Phillipian church from his prison cell! He wanted to express gratitude for sending him money. Why does he need money in jail you ask? I am thinking that it may be like today and I know there are those of you reading who are shouting out "canteen money." But I don't think Paul was trading cigarettes for Ramen Noodles!

Paul told them that his imprisonment was helping him to spread the gospel so maybe he was writing letters to other places and other inmates and needed to buy paper and pencils and stamps to mail those letters. Hmm...probably didn't have pencils in those days...and stamps? Who knows but he needed money for something.

Here is what it says in Phillipians as he wrote from a jail cell. Check this out;

"4 Rejoice in the Lord always; again I will say, rejoice. 5 Let your reasonableness be known to everyone. The Lord is at hand; 6 do not be anxious about anything, but in everything by prayer and supplication with thanksgiving let your requests be made known to God. 7 And the peace of God, which surpasses all understanding, will guard your hearts and your minds in Christ Jesus".

8 Finally, brothers, whatever is true, whatever is honorable, whatever is just, whatever is pure, whatever is lovely, whatever is commendable, if there is any excellence, if there is anything worthy of praise, think about these things. 9 What you have learned and received and heard and seen in me—practice these things, and the God of peace will be with you.

Think about it! He wrote it from jail, not some mansion. How much do you think these verses might help anxiety, depression, resentment, conflict and all things negative if we only could "think on the things he mentions?"

What I know for sure is that when you choose positive thoughts, you will find yourselves experiencing the "fruits of the spirit" talked about in Galatians 5:22-23, where it says, "But the fruit of the Spirit is love, joy, peace, patience, kindness, goodness, faithfulness, gentleness, self-control; against such things there is no law."

Can't you see those positive fruits hanging in your brain? Much more positive than the rotten potato! Speaking of rotten… I just thought of another analogy I heard this week. Read on…

WILL THAT THOUGHT
HELP YOU?
IF NOT, THROW IT AWAY
BUT KEEP THE DIAMONDS

DIAMOND GARBAGE

Garbage stinks. It is messy and gross and nobody in their right mind would dig through it....unless they knew there was something valuable in it.

So imagine for a moment that you were given an envelope of valuable diamonds. They were worth hundreds of thousands of dollars, but unfortunately, the envelope got mixed up with the junk mail and got tossed in the garbage.

So you head to the garbage truck and you find the envelope but it comes open and now the diamonds are intermingled with the garbage. What are you focusing on? The garbage, or are you focused on looking for the diamonds?

Much of what we focus on in our minds is garbage...not the things that we are grateful for, what we are good at, and the goals that we have set to accomplish.

Now you have the foundation for why I love each one of the 3 G's, and how they are consistent with the Christian faith. However, if all this Bible stuff is a little much for you, please don't quit reading because coming up is the scientific proof of why each one of these 3 G's has its own medical benefits in our brains and bodies if you actually use them.

FOOD FOR THOUGHT

1. What life experiences may have caused you to have toxic thoughts (rotten potatoes)?

    ____
    ____
    ____

2. Who do you turn to or where do you go for help when you are struggling?

    ____
    ____
    ____

3. What are the diamonds in your life that you can focus on? (You may have to dig for them)

    ____
    ____
    ____

4. Did you find some of the Bible verses to make sense and be helpful? If so which ones?

    ____
    ____
    ____

JOURNALING THE 3 G'S AND MORE

____
____
____
____
____
____
____
____

PART II

GOING DEEPER ON GRATITUDE

CHAPTER 6:

GRATITUDE: THE GATEWAY TO NEUROLOGICAL TRANSFORMATION

You have been given a quick overview of how the 3 G's help our brains but I wanted to give you an overview of each one of them specifically and how they individually impact your brain functioning and chemistry in different ways.

I have been a counselor for 35 years and the 3 G's is the most powerful, beneficial tool I have ever given to my clients.It is both scientifically based and has been proven to be effective for changing brain chemistry and mental, emotional, and even physical well being. It is kind of like giving your brain a warm hug.

Here are just a few of the studies on the first G, Gratitude, that prove my point;

"Keeping a gratitude journal causes less stress, improves the quality of sleep, and builds emotional awareness" (Seligman, Steen, Park, & Peterson, 2005).

"Grateful workers are more efficient, more productive and more responsible. Expressing gratitude in the workplace is a proactive action toward building interpersonal bonds and triggering feelings of closeness and bonding" (Algoe, 2012).

"People who express and feel gratitude have a higher volume of gray matter in the right inferior temporal gyrus" (Zahn et al., 2014).

Counting Blessings vs Burdens (Emmons & McCullough, 2003), a study conducted on evaluating the effect of gratitude on physical wellbeing, indicated that "16% of the patients who kept a gratitude journal, reported reduced pain symptoms, and were more willing to work out and cooperate with the treatment procedure."

University of California and University of Miami's study of undergraduate students indicated that "Participants who regularly engaged in recognizing and expressing gratitude experienced a significant increase in their overall sense of well-being." Specifically, they reported "considerably more satisfaction with their lives as a whole, felt more optimism about the upcoming week, and felt more connected with others" compared to the other groups.

The gratitude group also reported feeling more optimistic about their lives. They felt a heightened sense of joy and happiness. And a nice bonus – they experienced a greater willingness to help others.

In addition, they showed fewer symptoms such as headaches, muscle soreness, or feelings of fatigue and they felt more motivated to engage in healthy behaviors like exercise."

Clearly the scientific evidence exists that practicing gratitude is helpful but how does it actually work? I wondered that myself so I did a little research of my own so read on.

A FUN MEDICAL SCIENCE LESSON

Even though I like a lot of scientific stuff, it is also pretty detailed and requires way too much memory power for this 71-year-old ADHD brain to just spit out for you.

It can also get pretty boring if you just use all those medical mumbo-jumbo terms so I decided to find a fun way to explain what really goes on in the brain when you are practicing gratitude.

Here is the boring version;

Researchers have found that gratitude engages specific areas in the brain, such as the prefrontal cortex, anterior cingulate cortex, and areas within the reward circuitry like the ventral tegmental area (VTA) and nucleus accumbens. This interaction influences both our emotional responses and decision-making.

More fun!

I wanted to go a little deeper and understand more details but not that way, so here is my kind of version that goes along with my love of analogies...(with a little help from my comedic online faceless friends)

1. Prefrontal Cortex: Imagine this as the brain's ultimate life coach armed with a clipboard and to-do list. It's furiously organizing thoughts, prioritizing tasks, and every now and then, it blows a whistle when you're about to make a poor decision. Or, think of it as the meticulous librarian shushing your impulsive whims and reminding you to do your taxes or not react to those annoyances.
2. Anterior Cingulate Cortex- This is the brain's diplomatic Zen master. Picture it sitting cross-legged, calmly presenting two options like a game show host: "Behind door number one, serenity; and behind door number two, chaos." It's adept at teaching your brain to breathe in, breathe out, and maybe even do some yoga poses when handling emotional and cognitive juggling.
3. Ventral Tegmental Area (VTA) Consider this the brain's hype man. It's like the DJ at a party, dropping the beat (dopamine rush) just when you do something fantastic like eating chocolate or hitting a new personal best in your workout. It's always ready

with confetti cannons, cheering you on, "You loved it? Here's a mental high-five, go do it again!"

4. Nucleus Accumbens: Picture this as the happy-go-lucky thrill-seeker in your brain. It's always front row at the concert of life, waving a lighter and shouting for an encore. It's the one shouting "Yes!" when you've completed a level in your favorite game, rewarding you with a hit of satisfaction like a victory dance at the end of a workout montage.

And guess what chemical cocktail does gratitude stir up for your benefit? Some of the studies I mentioned have shown that practicing gratitude will

- Increase dopamine (motivation, reward, "this feels good, do it again")
- Increase serotonin (mood, well-being, calm)
- Increase oxytocin (connection, trust, bonding—especially in relationships)
- Sometimes boost endorphins (natural "feel good" chemicals, especially when gratitude is paired with movement, worship, or laughter)
- Decrease cortisol over time (lower stress, better emotional regulation)

So there's the good stuff! Now what happens to your brain when you are angry or negative and focusing on the rotten potatoes, or you are sitting in the muddy rut of negative thinking?

Research shows that when we're emotionally flooded or highly stressed, a few key things happen in the brain:

1. Reduced Activity in the Prefrontal Cortex.

Remember the life coach, organized librarian who keeps you on track, helps you stay calm and make good choices? Under stress, it "dims down," so it's harder to be logical, patient, or reasonable. You know what you *should* do, but at the moment, that part of the brain isn't fully online.

2. Fight-or-Flight Response Becomes Hard to Control

When the brain senses a threat (even an emotional one), your body can flip into fight-or-flight mode: racing heart, tense muscles, fast breathing. Without enough calming input from the thinking part of your brain, this reaction can feel way bigger than the situation really calls for—like your body is acting as if there's a tiger in the room when it's actually just an uncomfortable conversation.

3. Amygdala Takes the Lead

The amygdala is the brain's emotional alarm system. When stress is high and the thinking brain quiets down, the amygdala tends to take over.

That's when reactions can become very emotional, very fast, snapping, crying, wanting to escape, or feeling like everything is a huge deal. It's less "What's the wise response here?" and more "Get out of my way, I'm doing this."

4. Risk Assessment Gets Skewed

Because your rational brain isn't working at full strength, your sense of what's a "good idea" can get a little off. You might say things you normally wouldn't, send that text you'll regret later, or make choices that don't really line up with your values. In the moment, it can feel justified; later, it's often a "Why did I do that?" regret.

So now that you have a little better understanding of what's going on scientifically and medically in your body when you both practice gratitude, and the opposite, I'm going to ask you to consider doing a comprehensive list of EVERYTHING you can think of that you are grateful for.

I will be anxious to get your feedback on your list but I am guessing that 99.9% of you will not put on your gratitude list the top 3 things that some of the homeless people, like Chris, put on their lists.

RESCUE STORY # 6 CHRIS – HOMELESS WITH 6 HEART BY-PASSES AT 40 YEARS OLD

It was 2006 when we got the call from Salvation Army Homeless Shelter about Chris. He had been a drinker and smoker most of his life and along with a family history of trauma and abuse, it had taken its toll.

His health was deteriorating and he was having difficulty working at his job as a drafter for a construction company

He was given a random blood pressure test at their shelter and was immediately transported to the hospital where he came out of surgery less than 24 hours later with six bypasses in his heart.

He could not go back to the shelter because they were unable to provide care for him so he was in a hotel by himself trying to recover from this major open heart surgery.

We brought him into one of our homes and helped him to recover. Unfortunately, within a few months, two of his arteries had already clogged up again, and he had to have two stents put in.

It was a long process, but as Chris recovered, he became a great help in the home where he was living as a care provider.

Unfortunately, as time went on and his surgeries continued, he became addicted to the prescription medication. He also got into a relationship, got married and moved out, but the drug addiction destroyed that relationship and within a few years he ended up homeless again.

Chris came back to one of the sober homes he had been in before and rebuilt his life once again. He quit the drugs for good and remained sober.

Ralph and I had retired from that ministry in 2014, so we had not been that involved with Chris's life since he moved there, but we did keep in touch.

Eight years ago, the sober home where he was living was going to be sold and he had nowhere to go. We decided to invite him to move into our personal home in a spare bedroom we had and he has been here ever since.

He has had a total of 29 stents implanted to keep his heart beating along with many other surgeries.

He was going to be on the transplant list to get a new heart, but because he had a femoral artery aneurysm in the leg, they couldn't put him on the list.

In the meantime, his heart has completely (and miraculously, the doctors say) rewired itself, growing new pathways to keep it beating. They have now come up with a new procedure that he is eligible for but he doesn't want to miss work during the recovery time.

Despite all of these medical problems, Chris has continued to work at an assisted living facility these last 9 years where he was initially an activity aide. In the last year, there was a need for a driver, and he has been elevated to the transportation manager of the facility. He works about 20 hours a week to supplement his disability.

If it wasn't for his change of thinking that he was grateful to be alive, that he realized he was good enough to still have a purpose, and he had a goal to change lives every day, he simply would not be alive. He got off the proverbial pity pot and started to smell the roses in life instead of looking at the mess he had been sitting in.

There is always hope if you choose to never give up. Chris has rewired his brain into a new neural pathway just like his heart did and I really believe it was through his positive attitude and determination of being grateful every day to be alive and have an opportunity to serve others that he is here today being a blessing to the world.

Chris has lived as part of our family in our personal home now for the last 8 years and at times struggles financially. He, like the rest of us, is not only grateful for the miracle of being alive, but he is Grateful that we have never run out of toilet paper.

He has come to realize that despite failures, he is Good at being a blessing to others and his Goal is to get up and be productive every day, serving his elderly clients at the assisted living facility he works at, and live as long as he can.

IF YOU DON'T WANT
YOUR LIFE TO STINK
GET OFF THE PITY POT

WHAT'S ON YOUR GRATITUDE LIST?

In 2001, my husband, daughter, and I opened our sober house to homeless veterans. These men had been living outside in Wisconsin with the clothes on their backs and whatever they could carry in a garbage bag or suitcase.

It isn't so bad in Central Wisconsin in the summertime. The weather is tolerable and plenty of trees and grass to enjoy, sleep on and use for whatever you need it for, but in the winter...think about it. What would it be like to be needing to do your elimination business outside in a blizzard like this week with 40 degrees below zero windchills and 10" of snow.

We were grateful to be able to get these homeless veterans moved in where they had a chance at a fresh start. We asked them to make a Christmas list of what they still wanted or needed that they couldn't get for themselves because none of them had any income at all.

What do you think was on their wish list? The number one thing on their list was toilet paper. Yes you heard me TOILET PAPER!

Would you have put that on your gratitude list? Perhaps not right this moment, but next time you go to the bathroom and have to go number 2, the big dump, poo-poo or whatever you call it, I want you to think about getting up from that toilet, and not having any toilet paper. Feel that for a moment. Eeiu! Gross!

The second thing on our homeless people's lists was new underwear and the third thing was new jeans, for obvious reasons. They had lost their dignity and they just wanted some self-respect and clean clothes that weren't stained.

I remember crying when I read those lists—tears of heartbreak and humility. Forget gadgets and watches and a fancy meal at a nice restaurant. These men and women simply wanted dignity. This moment forever changed how I viewed gratitude and how much of a "pity pot" I was sitting on without realizing what I already had. How about you?

THANK GOD

FOR TOILET PAPER!

During the Covid-19 pandemic I started watching Dr. Andrew Huberman, an American neuroscientist, tenured professor at the Stanford University of Medicine and the host of the very popular "Huberman Lab Podcast."

Dr. Huberman is highly regarded for his research in brain development, neural plasticity, and visual system repair, and he hosts many amazing guests including Psychiatrist and author, Dr. Anna Lembke and best selling author, attorney and health podcaster, Rich Roll.

One year on Thanksgiving Dr. Huberman did a podcast on gratitude and he has some interesting research that encourages people to not just make a list. In fact, he says that listmaking isn't all that neurologically effective if you don't feel it emotionally.

Here are a couple of highlights in my less than professorish way of speaking and hopefully still capturing the essence of Dr. Huberman's Podcast on gratitude.

1. Gratitude is not just a random feeling that shows up uninvited like, "Hey, I'm grateful today!" It's more like a mental muscle you can strengthen through practice and daily workouts.
2. Recalling things that spark joy for you automatically changes direction for your brain from being negative to being positive. You're basically telling your brain: "Hi, we're going to focus on safety, support, and reward signals now, not threat alarms and doom scrolling." That shift can move your nervous system away from rumination, scarcity, and resentment.
3. Gratitude helps our brain to constantly be updating by asking ourselves "What matters? What repeats? What predicts relief?" It helps train your brain to notice what's worth repeating.
4. Gratitude helps put a sticky note on life experiences as worth paying attention to. Over time, gratitude teaches that life has value even though it is stressful and even if things aren't perfect there are things that are worth living for and hanging on to.

5. Gratitude helps us stay more mellow and less reactive. Emotions aren't random lightning bolts, they're influenced by attention, interpretation, and memory cues. Gratitude tells our mind to just chill out and focus on the good stuff instead of focusing on what bugs us which will help us feel a little more serene
6. Gratitude can reduce your tendency to be a pitbull when someone or something comes at you in uncomfortable ways. Think of it as a mental "recalibration" button: we are not currently in immediate danger. (Even if your inbox is trying its best to convince you.)
7. Gratitude is a great substitute for a sleeping pill because when you look back at your day focusing on all the things you are grateful for it helps to calm your nervous system and help you sleep. It reduces the "clutter" so your brain can take a nap.
8. Gratitude is linked with meaning and purpose. Huberman often distinguishes between momentary pleasure and deeper meaning because gratitude takes you outside of yourself and focuses on other things, people, supports and purpose.
9. Gratitude works best when you get specific things like more plot and less postcards. Instead of "I am grateful for a roof over my head." look at all the things under the roof and say "I am grateful for my home, heat, running water, a comfy bed, hot water, TV, etc etc etc.... "You could list hundreds of things if you walk around and look and all of them help your brain!
10. Be sure to let others give because the greatest benefits come when you let other people give to you so instead of just saying " thanks for the coffee" you say "I am so grateful that you took time out of your busy day to consider me and bring some of my favorite kind of coffee! I am so blessed!."
11. Be real. Don't just fake it! Let yourself feel it both when you give and when you receive. The more you do the better you will feel.

Dr. Hubermans also said "You don't need to do this every day like it's flossing for your soul.

1 to 3 times a week is enough to drive neuroplastic changes—because your brain learns through repetition, not through exhaustion."

HMMM.... Now, no disrespect to Dr. Huberman because I know he is a real scientist and I am not, but my experience beckons to differ with him on this one... I want my soul flossed every day... Every time I am feeling like my spiritual teeth are all gunked up, I want to be flossing with the gratitude flosser because I witnessed that the more my clients can practice gratitude, the better their day goes.

Overall I think Dr. Huberman is brilliant and you can find him talking about tons of neuroscientific stuff on YouTube or other platforms so look him up! He also has a book coming out in September of 2026 and you can order it on Amazon. It is called Protocols: An Operating Manual for the Human Body by Andrew D. Huberman Ph.D.

RESCUE STORY #7 TROY – THE VIETNAM VET WITH A 30 YEAR PRISON SENTENCE WHO BECAME THE 1ST BLACK BUSINESS OWNER IN WAUSAU, WI

Troy was a Vietnam Veteran who had been shot during the war and was given morphine for pain as was the custom during those days. He became addicted to it because of physical pain to begin with but eventually, the PTSD, the challenge of reintegration and being disabled led him to use it because of emotional pain. Eventually, the addiction got the best of him and he ended up being arrested for robbery and possession of drugs.

He had not actually even entered the building that was robbed, but they decided that since they felt he had orchestrated the break-in (and he was the black guy from out of town) that they had to come down hard. The white guys who actually did the robbery got probation, Troy got sentenced to 30 years in prison.

Appeal after appeal finally got his sentence reduced to 13 years since the higher courts found he was the victim of "cruel and unusual punishment."

Troy was immediately referred to our Reintegration and Assistance Program RAP for veterans and others in recovery. His parole officer had hopes that we could help him transition while also ensuring that he was staying clean and sober.

Troy came with a plan but as a black man in a primarily white city who had originally gotten a 30-year sentence for drugs and robbery, he didn't think he had much of a chance, but he had a lot going for him. He took advantage of being in prison and became a licensed minister, created an artistic greeting card business and helped others.

Troy had also developed a business plan for opening the " Hot Diggity Dog" food stand that included a unique variety of hotdog fixings that he was sure would be a hit in this northern Wisconsin town.

His hopes were dashed when his probation officer told him he could not operate a hotdog stand because he was a convicted drug felon and children might come to the hotdog stand so he needed to prove himself first.

As part of our program, we helped people to rebuild their reputations so we got Troy involved with a supportive business working in a restaurant that was operated by the VFW (Veterans of Foreign Wars.)

Troy was an amazing worker and highly appreciated which continually improved his reputation and got him closer to his goal of owning his own hotdog stand.

He was a shining example of using the 3 G's to be Grateful for the opportunity that he had. He was able to gain experience in a restaurant by showing what he was Good at. He also took advantage of getting to know people in the community that would support him in his Goal of starting his own business.

He was able to see himself as a gifted and talented man of God that had been called to be tested to wait a little longer to implement the dream God had given him.

His goal was to just continue staying clean and sober and follow everything he needed to do to gain his true freedom to run his own life again. He did it!

As we have experienced in the past God provided things for our residents in ways we had never thought of and it was a confirmation to Troy that his dream would come true.

The first thing was that we received a call from a local business owner who supported our mission and he had a mobile food stand that was for sale. He agreed to give us a great deal on it if it would help our organization and this veteran have a chance to move forward.

To give us even more confirmation that this was meant to be, we received a referral for our program and Pete happened to have just come from a carnival tour where he operated a food stand! He got us going on using the stand to raise funds until Troy was ready to buy it.

Two years after his release from prison, Troy became the first African-American business owner in Wausau Wisconsin. He successfully ran this business for several years before selling it and moving to be with his family in another state.

Troy passed away a few years later, but the power of the 3 G's and giving people HOPE which I define as Help, Opportunity, Praise, and Encouragement, is evident in his life and story.

Perhaps you have a past or are even sitting in your present situation wondering if there will ever be a future for you. This is proof that yes! There is always HOPE... you may just need a little Help-Opportunity-Praise-Encouragement and the humility to ask for it.

What have you been waiting for that you thought wasn't possible? Think about it, pray about it, then write it down and get going on it.

FOOD FOR THOUGHT

1. What do you think your mission or purpose is on this earth?

2. Do you feel you are living it to the best of your ability or are you stuck?

3. What negative thoughts or behaviors come to mind that limit you from living your God-given purpose?

4. What action can you take today to move forward with a more positive mindset?

JOURNALING THE 3 G'S AND MORE

CHAPTER 7:

THE ENTITLEMENT TRAP

PASTOR BONIGALA SAM DANIELS

Entitlement is a sneaky little thief. It steals joy, hides blessings, and whispers, *"You deserve more."* But here's a little secret: entitlement and gratitude can't coexist. It's like trying to mix oil and water—they'll never blend.

During the pandemic, I was contacted by Pastor Bonigala Sam Daniels from India through his ministry, Rafa Blessings Ministry India on Facebook. I normally don't respond to men at all but after checking out his profile I felt led to respond and ask him why he was contacting me, fully expecting a request for donations.

To my surprise he responded with "I was praying and God led me to you, and the Holy Spirit wouldn't leave me alone until I reached out and asked you to speak live on my facebook page."

I was shocked but excited and every Saturday for the last 5 years I have gone live on Facebook for Pastor Daniels and all the people he and many other people all over the world have shared with others.

Now, since Facebook decided to delete live videos after 30 days, I am going live on YouTube where you can find me at @lindalarsonschlitz to get notifications.

Through Pastor Daniels, I have witnessed firsthand what true gratitude looks like—even when there seems to be little to be grateful for. He is an example of faith during hard times, that is for sure!

I had been speaking on his page for several months when he reached out asking for help for the "slum pastors" who were in desperate need of food for their families and congregations. Covid-19 was wreaking havoc and they had no jobs, no food and they didn't have health insurance like we do here in the United States or so many other places.

Pastor Daniels asked me if I could please help to buy rice to sustain them as that was the cheapest way to stay alive. So a few days later, 10 pastors and volunteers traveled up to 20 miles on foot or by bicycle just to receive a single bag of rice. Though my donation was a mere $200 to give them each one bag of rice, their reaction was anything but small.

These pastors came together and celebrated as if they had received a feast from heaven. They hung a large sign with my name on it, held a special service, and even video-called me to express their thanks. Some of them with tears in their eyes called me an angel and a blessing that had "saved lives."

Meanwhile, I sat in my comfortable home, in tears myself, suddenly ashamed of the ease with which Amazon Prime delivers my quinoa and chocolate cravings in 24 hours!

We are very spoiled here in the United States and it would serve us well to consider the Bible verse "It is more blessed to give than to receive" in Acts 20:35.

And, how about the golden rule that is in two different places in the Bible Luke 6:31: "And as you wish that others would do to you, do so to them."

Consider Matthew 7:12 "So whatever you wish that others would do to you, do also to them, for this is the Law and the Prophets."

Can you imagine what your life would be like when all you have is rice and water to sustain you? What would it be like to not be able to turn on the faucet and get water and have to walk to get it and then boil it to be sure it is safe to drink?

Today when you look at the food you are blessed to consume, the home you live in, the car you drive, the health care you have access to, and the other countless blessings you have taken for granted, (like toilet paper) take a moment and think about considering what you can do to help those that are less fortunate. It will help your brain. (More on that in another chapter.)

HOPE FOR LOVE- WE CAN MAKE IT HAPPEN IF WE STAY CONNECTED

Relationships are hard. At least they can be, but gratitude works wonders there, too. One of my favorite mantras is this: *Expectations are premeditated resentments.*

Think about the last time you got angry. Do you have it in your mind? Somebody did something you didn't want them to do, or, they didn't do something you wanted them to do and you got angry. Right?

Does that mean we shouldn't ever expect anything from anyone?

Well, go ahead and have expectations, but if you are attaching your emotional well being to something you can't control (another human being's behavior, or even the weather) you set yourself up for a world of hurt, or getting stuck in a muddy rut of self pity and let me tell you, being on the pity pot is not fun! (especially if you have no toilet paper! LOL)

But seriously, think about it for a minute. How often do we focus on what is good in a relationship instead of what we don't like? He goes to work every day, comes home every night, bought you a beautiful card and took you out to dinner on your anniversary but he didn't get you flowers and you are all wound up about it.

If you wouldn't have expected him to put his love in some imaginary box that he needed to wrap in just a perfect sort of way or a bouquet of flowers (which you more than likely didn't even tell him that you wanted) to prove to you he loves you, you wouldn't be so upset.

Gratitude softens hearts and builds bridges. It's the WD-40 for the squeaky wheels of marriage, friendships, and family ties.

Let the expectations go and be grateful for every minute you have with your loved ones. Focus on what they are doing right, not what they are doing that you don't like.

Unfortunately, from the time we are born we are being compared to others. The Apgar score tells our parents if we are "normal" or not. We are judged from that point on (more on that later) but we have to fight against the social construct we have of comparison and negativity.

Look at how many people trash their spouses and everyone else on social media. Those are the things that go viral, but making the change to focus on the positive can save relationships, families, businesses, and much more. We choose to pay it forward.

Whether it is your partner, your kids, your co-workers or anyone else you are in a relationship with, focus on what you are grateful for and let them know and it will make a difference in your brain and theirs.

EXPECTATIONS ARE
PREMEDITATED
RESENTMENTS

RESCUE STORY #8 TOM – THE SUPERINTENDANT

Tom scheduled an appointment because he was stressed out going to school every day and having the staff and students complaining about things. He had been in the school system for 30 years and he hated the changes he was seeing. He expected things to go a certain way and they weren't.

His negative attitude had spilled over to home and his wife and kids were walking on eggshells. He was angry more often than not and it had to change. He just didn't know how. He felt his expectations were reasonable so what was the problem?

He accepted the challenge of doing the comprehensive list of 3 G's and since he was a man of faith he was accustomed to practicing gratitude but the Good at and Goals were a little more challenging, especially at home.

He engaged his wife (who had told him he needed to go to counseling because he was really hurting the family,) and she gladly joined in. They brought their teenage kids into the exercise of the 3 G's and things improved a great deal.

As he went through each day at school with "expectations are pre-meditated resentments" in his mind he was able to let go of what he was hoping people would do. He also did some real soul searching about whether this was a good fit for him any longer.

He got up each morning setting goals to be positive by practicing gratitude for new beginnings and once he decided to change courses and get a dream job he was able to get excited about the future rather than dread it.

He quit making excuses that he was too busy at work to do family things and went on a bucket list trip with the family. He used the "what's the worst thing that could happen" test to all the things he thought was on his must do list and realized some of them didn't have to be done at all.

By the end of our 8 months of meeting together he had ended the year, bought a new dream home in a town where he found his dream job and I am hoping they are living happily ever after.

By using the 3 G's he realized life or even his job wasn't so terrible and he could be Grateful for everything each day. He saw that he was Good at things and that he could find another job and that he could change by setting Goals each day to take control of his toxic thoughts while creating a new neural pathway.

FOOD FOR THOUGHT:

1. Think of the last time you got angry…what were your expectations?

2. What could you have thought differently about things to prevent the anger?

3. Does it benefit you to have expectations if you can't control the person or thing you are putting those expectations on?

4. How can you think differently when someone doesn't meet your expectations so you can feel emotionally well about it.

JOURNALING THE 3 G'S AND MORE

CHAPTER 8:

HOW TO MAKE GRATITUDE YOUR LIFESTYLE WITH MORE GOOD BOOK ADVICE

Gratitude isn't just a list you write before bed. It's a mindset shift, a lens through which you view the world. It's saying, "Thank you for what I have, even when life's messy."

If you are a Christian (or even if you aren't) the Bible laid the foundation for why we should practice gratitude long before neuroscientists figured out it was good for us.

There are between 130-150 Bible verses about gratitude or giving thanks, which is certainly a lot of encouragement to do something that has now been proved to be scientifically beneficial.

I am going to share a few of my favorite gratitude verses, and if you can remember back to English class I want you to pay attention to the sentence structure.

Now, Miss Lucas would probably tell you that I did not do well when it came to knowing a conjunction from an interjection, or a predicate nominative but I did know a verb which was an action word, and an adverb which is like a news reporter describing the "how, when, where, why and to what extent" of the verb.

For example: I Thessalonians 5:18 says *"Give thanks* in <u>all</u> circumstances; for this is God's will for you in Christ Jesus."

The directive is to "give thanks" and the when is "in all circumstances." Not some circumstances or if we feel like it, but all the time.

We have talked about this one before, but since we seem to need reminders, Philippians 4:6-7 says "Do not be anxious about ANYTHING but in EVERY situation, by prayer and petition, with thanksgiving, present your requests to God and the peace of God which surpasses ALL understanding will keep your hearts and minds on Christ."

Here is another scripture verse that is quite clear about what you need to do. It sounds a little parental. When mom or dad said "do not" that usually didn't mean, unless you don't want to do it!

Here we are instructed to "not be anxious" about ANYTHING. You ask when, and it says in EVERY SITUATION.

Again, be aware that whenever there is an instruction or directive given it will be followed with a "so that" consequence or reward. In this verse the so that is "that we will receive the peace of God which surpasses ALL understanding."

One more, which is similar to the first one, is Ephesians 5:20b which says, " giving thanks ALWAYS and for EVERYTHING to God the Father in the name of our Lord Jesus Christ."

Always give thanks in everything. Well ok... I'll admit... those are impossible... We can't do it perfectly but my Bible college professor Dr. Martin explained that the word perfect in the Greek actually means " complete" and went on to say that when we are doing our best we are as perfect as we are going to be.

The larger context of Jesus's teaching was that by trusting him we are "complete." Here is my favorite verse...again.

Romans 12:2: says "Do not be conformed to this world, but be transformed by the renewal of your mind, that by testing you may discern what is the will of God, what is good and acceptable and perfect."

Let's pick this one apart a little as it relates to gratitude;

1 "Do not conform to this world, but be transformed by the renewal of your mind."

If your parents say "don't run out in traffic" they don't mean, unless you want to. They mean DO NOT run out in traffic.

Paul is giving the Philippian church, and the rest of us the same directive- DO NOT conform... BE transformed...RENEW your mind

Notice in the verses I am going to share throughout this book that most of them start with a verb.

A verb is an action word which is something we must do.

What about not conforming? What does that mean?

To not conform means you live by YOUR values, even if everyone else is doing the hokey pokey and turning themselves around, because *you* know that's NOT what it's all about.

There is a social norm of drinking, using drugs, getting angry, calling names, using violence, profanity, escaping into social media or lots of other things as a coping mechanism, but Peter points out that we can renew our minds instead. And now, you can use these verses and the 3 Gs to renew yours.

HOW TO REJOICE WHEN YOU ARE SAD AND GRIEVING

I understand there are some things that seem impossible to do that the Bible talks about. Like this verse we just went over from Phillipians 4:4 where it says to "Rejoice in the Lord always. Again I say, rejoice."

Paul has to say it twice to make sure we get it. Clearly he knew that we are slow learners and need repetition.

Yes this means rejoice when you're out of coffee, rejoice when you lose your job, rejoice when there is sickness and death. But how? Why?

It doesn't mean we never grieve. Jesus wept when his friend Lazarus died but that quickly turned to rejoicing when he had the faith to believe that God had a bigger plan that would give people hope and he raised him from the dead.

Perhaps you don't believe in heaven and life after death. I choose to believe because it makes me feel better but if you don't, what I can tell you is that the pain does get better, especially if you can focus on the things you are learning in this book.

I will also challenge you, that if you are grieving the loss of someone who has died or is no longer in your life for some reason, to try just asking whoever is up there (I choose to call Him God) to send a sign that will assure you that their spirit lives on.

One of my client's young son died and he collected rocks so she started praying for a sign and very soon she began finding rocks shaped in the form of a heart. I cried along with her when she found one on Mother's Day the first year after he died.

She transformed her mind that day and she was able to be grateful for something for the first time since he died. She now has a collection of heart shaped rocks.

Making these kinds of perspective changes is the only way to not be stuck in the muddy ruts of pain, grief, anger, hurt and resentment. Consider giving it a try.

NO ONE CAN MAKE YOU MAD WITHOUT YOUR PERMISSION

RESCUE STORY # 9 – PETE AND PENNY – EXHAUSTED, FRUSTRATED PARENTS OF TEENS

It was Penny who came to me first. She was in tears, exhausted after working a 40 hour work week and coming home to chaos with three teenagers who refused to do anything except demand.

Pete was a quiet man who also worked a lot of hours and didn't know how to support Penny. He would ask the kids to help and they would say they would but then they didn't.

By the time I began meeting with them, there was so much hurt, anger, and resentment that they needed help finding hope and a starting point.

Using the 3 G's to begin to appreciate each other, and what they were bringing to their relationship, and their kids lives, was a first step to focus on what they were grateful for, what each member of the family brought to the table, and what goals they were hoping to accomplish in therapy, and in their household.

Once Penny and Pete realized it was important that the kids saw what was under the anger and nagging, and they began sharing their feelings, it made a difference.

Penny shared with the kids that she was so exhausted that it was affecting her health. She stated that she needed them and she knew that they had skills and abilities that she didn't have or didn't have time to use.

The whole family did the 3 Gs together. First, they worked together to write down a list of as many things as they could think about to be grateful for. Things that were privileges and not rights.

Since electronics were a big point of contention, having the kids realize that having any access at all to electronics was a gift and not a right that they should take for granted and expect, gave them a change in perspective.

The parents gave the kids some choices about who might want to do what tasks that needed to be done. They had tried assigning things but they found that telling teenagers what to do wasn't very effective, so giving them options and choices made a big difference.

Penny and Pete returned a couple weeks later, shocked at the cooperation that they were getting as they focused on being grateful for what their kids were now doing and they committed to continue to affirm the kids in their cooperation.

The entire family grew closer and were more appreciative and engaged with one another, and the house was getting cleaned up, which made everybody happy.

FOOD FOR THOUGHT

1. What is the main thing you got out of this chapter?

   ____
   ____
   ____

2. What areas do you feel that you may be taking things for granted in your life?

   ____
   ____
   ____

3. Are there any areas where you tend to sit on the pity pot?

   ____
   ____
   ____

4. What areas do you think you may be conforming to the world that aren't good for you?

   ____
   ____
   ____

JOURNALING THE 3 G'S AND MORE

____
____
____
____
____
____
____
____
____

PART III

THE POWER OF ACKNOWLEDGING YOUR GOD-GIVEN STRENGTHS

CHAPTER 9:

WHAT ARE YOU GOOD AT?

I have never had a client who hasn't reported that this is the hardest of the 3 G's to do. We seem to think that acknowledging what we are good at is bragging.

We also have a problem that people seem to notice what we are doing "wrong" rather than what we are good at. More on this later but let's get started with the good.

I always encourage people to write down what they feel they are Good at, but then also to ask their friends, their family, their coworkers, their teachers and anyone they know what they think that they are Good at. There are inevitably other people that see things in you that you don't.

For example, if you are reading this, you can write on your Good at list that

1. You are resilient because whatever you have been through, you have made it to this point.

2. You are humble enough to know that you need help and are looking to this book to find some.
3. You are curious and open because you are considering something you didn't know before and are contemplating trying it.
4. You are a perspective shifter because you have taken the time to look at a different point of view

I don't even know you, yet it is easy to see your strengths. Please put those down on your list, and then feel them. Look in the mirror and tell yourself these positive qualities and let yourself feel good about it.

In my 35 years as a counselor and now a life coach, the 3 G's have been a great tool. Here is another one of the stories that demonstrates its power. Please read on to learn how this actually works in your brain and life.

RESCUE STORY #10 – JIM, THE RICH BUSINESS OWNER

Jim was the owner of a multimillion-dollar business. He was successful, confident in his abilities at work, and, by all accounts, had "made it."

But despite his corner office and impressive bank account, he found himself feeling discontent and anxious at work and downright depressed at home. And the worst part? He had no idea why.

I suggested he start journaling using the "3 G's"—a simple exercise where he lists:

1. What he's **Grateful** for,
2. What he's **Good at**, and
3. What **Goals** he can work toward.

I also encouraged him to bring his family in on the fun. (Because, let's be honest, self-improvement is way easier when you've got backup.)

Jim, however, was skeptical. "I'm not one of those touchy-feely people," he grumbled. And to be fair, I hear that a lot—especially from men, who sometimes act like acknowledging emotions will somehow revoke their membership in the "Brotherhood of Tough Guys."

But here's the thing: bottling up feelings doesn't make them disappear. It just makes them pop up in unexpected places—like stress headaches, late-night fridge raids, or raging at the TV, (or your family) when your sports team is losing, or worse the station starts buffering because of unstable internet.

Deep down, Jim was afraid to look too closely at his feelings because he thought he was failing at life, and he secretly hoped there was a magic pill that would make everything better.

And while medication can absolutely help with anxiety and depression, his problem was bigger than that—it wasn't just about brain chemistry; it was about mindset.

For weeks, Jim avoided introducing the 3 G's to his family. "They won't be into it," he insisted. "Especially my boys. No way."

I told him about another parent who had such success with the 3 G's that his young kids refused to get out of the car for school until they'd done them because they wanted to start the day with confidence, set their goals, and remind themselves what they were grateful for.

That got his attention, so, reluctantly, Jim gave it a shot on the morning drive to school.

At first, it was awkward. (What life-changing thing isn't?) But after a couple of days, his kids started taking turns sharing their 3 G's. Then, something unexpected happened.

When it was Jim's turn to say what he was good at, he could not think of one thing. He seriously was at a loss and just then his three kids jumped in before he could answer.

"You're a great dad."
"You do stuff with us."
"You take us to school."
"You encourage us."
"You buy us stuff."

Jim's ego, which he thought was tough as steel, suddenly felt a little fragile.

He found himself choking up—not over some grand accomplishment, but over something so simple: his kids appreciated him.

The power of the 3 G's had snuck up on him, strengthening his bond with them and making him realize that even the mundane parts of parenting mattered.

After a few weeks, something amazing happened. Jim felt good about himself—not just at work, but at home. He gained confidence in his role as a dad. He saw his work as an opportunity to help others.

And his wife? He started cherishing her in a way he never had before and guess what, she responded in all sorts of positive ways that brought them much closer.

It didn't take much longer before he felt he had a handle on his mental and emotional well being and we ended therapy as a success.

LOOK FOR THE GOOD-
LET GO OF WHAT
ANNOYS YOU

YOUR TURN

Of course, for those who struggle with self-worth, this exercise can feel downright painful but as you can see, asking your loved ones for help can make it an encouragement instead of a pain.

People worry, "What if no one can think of anything good about me?" But time and time again, I've seen people hear more positive things than they ever would've dared to write down themselves.

I even had one guy say, "yes I got a lot of positive comments from others but what if I think they are wrong and I don't agree with their positive assessment of me?"

WOW! What does that say? I told him he could reject any negative comments but not the positive perceptions that others have of him.

When I have clients do this exercise, I've seen grown adults—with jobs, mortgages, and perfectly functional poker faces—tear up when they finally see themselves in a positive light.

And yes, making a list of what you're good at can feel uncomfortable at first, but it's a crucial step in rewiring a negative mindset because, if you don't believe you're capable of change, you won't make it happen.

But here's the good news: You can do this. Read on to discover the scientific proof that focusing on what you are good at changes your brain chemistry.

GOD DIDN'T MAKE NORMAL "WE ARE FEARFULLY AND WONDERFULLY MADE"

Jeremiah 29:11

FOOD FOR THOUGHT

1. What are you Good at?

2. Who can you ask to help you with expanding your list?

3. Are there things other people think you are good at that you don't?

4. What changes can you make to focus more on your strengths vs. your weaknesses?

JOURNALING THE 3 G'S AND MORE

CHAPTER 10:

HOW SELF-AFFIRMATION HEALS AND REWIRES YOUR BRAIN

HOW TO HACK YOUR BRAIN AND MAKE IT LISTEN

Most people who struggle with alcohol (or any addiction or mental illness) already know how to beat themselves up. The inner critic is loud, familiar, and—if we're honest—sometimes feels more "true" than anything kind or hopeful we might say to ourselves.

But the truth is, your brain was never designed to be fueled by shame. God wired your brain to respond to truth, love, and purpose. When you practice self-affirmation rooted in who God says you are and what He created you for, you're not just "being positive." You are literally engaging brain circuits and chemicals that help you heal, make better choices, and stay healthy, clear minded, and it's much easier to make good decisions like staying clean and sober, eating responsibly and so much more.

Like the previous chapters where I showed you how our brain chemistry is changed by focusing on Gratitude, I want to show you how thinking about what you are Good at impacts your brain in equally as powerful, but different ways.

When you practice self-affirmation, you're basically hacking your brain into being kinder to you. It reduces stress, boosts confidence, and makes you more likely to go after what you want. Plus, it keeps those negative tapes in your head from being too loud and messing up your serenity

If you have ever stood in front of a mirror and tried to say, "I am an awesome, intelligent, talented, loved, wonderfully created human, while your brain whispered, "Yeah right…take a look at your life, you are a mess, then congratulations, you've already met your nervous system.

Our internal messages that have become a part of our subconscious mind can actually be reprogrammed but we have to know how to get rid of those nasty "viruses" that have plagued us for years, bringing down self-esteem and our perceptions of ourselves.

Having been diagnosed with ADHD in my 20's and having the constant channel changing in my brain, I understood my friend Joe perfectly when he described his brain chaos as dealing with the "committee" in his head and they are all talking at once. Like most committees, some members are helpful, and some just like creating drama!

That is how our brain is. It is an awesome organ but did you ever notice how we crave things that might not be good for us? That is because new research has shown that the brain's reward system is in the same part of the brain as the pain center which presents some obvious challenges.

Remember in the chapter on Gratitude, I talked about the PFC (Prefrontal Cortex), and I shared the analogy of "the boss" or the "librarian" that is the decision-making part of your brain that helps to make choices, giving you that nudge when you are heading in the wrong direction and perhaps making a bad choice?

Well the good thing is that the PFC also will remind you that you are doing an awesome job when you make that good decision to acknowledge your successes. It is like your personal life coach that is there cheering you on and getting you back on track back to homeostasis.

Another part of the brain that is impacted is the Anterior Cingulate Cortex (ACC) as "the Worry Wart" which deals with conflict and self-doubt, but is also the Zen master (or like my mom said, the angel on your shoulder.) It will help you to chill out, be kind to yourself and manage those negative voices (the devil on the other shoulder) that are trying to bring you down.

The ACC helps you get to the point where you can say “I messed up, but I'm loved” which helps to limit emotional distress.

A challenging brain function is the conflicting function of the Default Mode Network (DMN) because this is your brain's ‘background storyteller’ which is active when you're daydreaming, remembering, or thinking about yourself and contemplating your life.

It becomes very active when you're replaying memories, judging yourself, or imagining how others see you. When things are unhealthy, the DMN can get stuck in rumination: looping over failures, hurts, and worries—often fueling shame (“I'm not enough,” “I'm broken,” “I'll never change”).

The good news is that when you intentionally practice healthier, truth-based self-talk and affirmations, reflect on your strengths, and see your life as a growing, redemptive story, you're still using the DMN—but now to “renew the mind” instead of attack it.

Over time, this conscious shift can change your brain's default (automatic response) from “What's wrong with me?” to “I'm learning, growing, and my life has purpose.”

Unfortunately, this is an uphill battle in our society because even our doctors and nurses in the birthing room set out to see what is “wrong” with us based on the APGAR scale, which measures whether we are “normal” or not the minute we pop out of the womb.

Appearance**:** Skin color (pink, blue, or pale)

Pulse: Heart rate (absent, less than 100 beats per minute, or more than 100 beats per minute)

Grimace**:** Reflex irritability (no response, grimace, or cry)

Activity**:** Muscle tone (limp, some flexion, or active movement)

Respiration: Breathing effort (absent, slow and irregular, or strong and regular)

- **7-10:** Normal
- **4-6:** May require additional medical attention
- **0-3:** Indicates a serious medical emergency

I had never thought about it until I looked at this chart for the first time since my daughter was born 44 years ago. As you can see from the very beginning, we were judging skin color as "normal" or not. I realize it is different for every race but somehow we have brought that whole thing into our society. Her skin color was not "normal" because she had yellow jaundice.

And what do we say to ourselves when we are "below average"? Synonyms are things like "below, beneath, under, down, lower, behind and bottom. How does that make you feel?

At this moment I am at the Chicago Airport with a 5 hour delay in my flight, so I have asked some random people what was the first thing that came to mind if they were told they were "below average." The first lady said "trailer trash" the second one said "disappointment" others said "shame," "guilt", "embarrassed," and "angry."

A very interesting response came from siblings from Alaska. The sister said she would say to the person "you don't know me" and her brother responded by saying "you are wrong."

Remember our thoughts cause feelings so if we get an assignment back in school like I did when I was little and the first thing you see is a bunch of red check marks you literally see red. Red is not good, it makes you mad because it says you weren't "good enough" because good enough was if you saw a big 100% at the top of the page.

Even though "average" was supposedly good enough, somewhere along the line the expectation has changed and now we have to be better than the majority of the rest of the people in the world.

In the United States about 68% of the population has an "average IQ" score. Yet, we are expected to do above average work, to get into college, to gain more knowledge so we can get an above average salary. An average salary doesn't even support most families these days... does that make sense to you?

The sad thing is that the assessments for all of those things don't take into account how things like trauma, family dynamics, income, living situations, and more impacts a person's ability to learn.

For example, studies show that poverty and the stress from financial insecurity can decrease cognitive function, sometimes by as many as 13 IQ points. Louisiana has the lowest IQ scores in the United States but they also have a high poverty rate, and its median household income is significantly lower than the national average.

In the United States people have been murdered because of their opinions about whether it is "fair" that we consider some of these issues when admitting people into college. The diversity, equity, and inclusion initiatives and the Equal Rights laws in the US open opportunities to people who may not have had the chance that others had to "make the grade."

We need to embrace our differences and the amazing gifts, talents, abilities, interests and experiences that God has blessed us with. If we can only realize all we have done to help others and the impact we have had on others over the years, and can do so in the future, we can impact our brain chemistry to have the motivation to change.

Niron, one of the veterans that we worked with who came to us ready to end his life, truly re-routed his brain chemistry to become a real blessing to others.

RESCUE STORY #11 – NIRON, THE HOMELESS VETERAN

Niron called me late one night and I could tell he was crying. It was cold outside here in Northcentral Wisconsin and he was homeless. His wife had just left him for another man, and he was devastated. She kicked him out .He had no place to go.

Knowing that I ran a program for homeless veterans, he reached out and asked if we had room for him. He had no job, no money, and no hope. He had been drinking to manage his feelings, but it wasn't effective and since we had a sober house, alcohol was not allowed.

He had some learning problems in school but he had done OK in life overall and even was accepted into the Army. His mental health problems got the best of him when he was sent overseas and he had a breakdown and was discharged.

Unfortunately, they determined that his mental illness was pre-existing and because he was a "peacetime veteran" with only 1 year and 10 months in he did not qualify for VA benefits of any kind.

By the time he got to us he had been diagnosed with anxiety, depression and diabetes and those had gotten worse because of his drinking and lack of self-care. He was divorced, estranged from his kids and was also overweight and felt he had no purpose anymore.

Our program had just opened a secondhand store so the residents could learn some new skills and help to generate income to pay for the overhead costs so they did not have to get an outside job.

Many, like Niron, were having difficulty getting anyone to hire them. Some of the residents had criminal records or a very bad work history.

Niron was more than willing to help out with our new venture, but he was limited in his mobility, but he was very willing to log the inventory of the 3,000 books that had been donated by a Korean veteran to our secondhand store. It was no small task and it took him quite a while, but he was happy to do it and help to set up the book store.

He also learned how to work the cash register, serve customers, and eventually helped to train and manage people. He did have computer skills so as the program grew, he helped with managing some of the paperwork and then started selling merchandise online.

He realized he was really enjoying computers, so I helped him get into the technical college for a computer degree. He remained with us until he graduated with an associate degree in computer support, and in the meantime, I had also assisted him in getting disability as his health and mobility were deteriorating because of diabetic neuropathy.

He was the first one to graduate from our rehabilitation education and training program. He moved out into his own apartment where he lived until he died of diabetic complications a few years later.

He had been one of the people that helped to lead doing the 3 G's every morning with all the other residents and was on the front lines of marketing and fundraising in the community.

His life is an example of the 3 G's in action and receiving HOPE which again Is Help Opportunity, Praise and Encouragement. In an interview he did for a marketing video he explained that what we did for him through the many services and counseling was to not give him a hand out but a hand up.

FOOD FOR THOUGHT

1. What are some of the negative messages you have in your mind that have led you to feel you are "not normal"?

2. What things do you need to do to look at your strengths instead of your weaknesses?

3. What message stands out to you the most from this chapter?

4. How did Niron's story impact your thinking?

JOURNALING THE 3 G'S AND MORE

CHAPTER 11:

NEGATIVITY BIAS

HOW DID WE GET THIS NEGATIVE?

Dr Eica Musser, Ph.D., of Florida International University did a research project on parental criticism of ADHD children and found that by the age of 10 ADHD kids often hear 20,000 more negative comments than positive affirmations.

Self-esteem expert Jack Canfield, of *Chicken Soup for the Soul*, talks about the impact on self esteem in children and found, as I did when I was a school counselor, that children who entered school with healthy self esteem progressively had lower scores the older they got.

While renowned relationship researcher Dr. John Gottman established a 5:1 "magic ratio" for positive-to-negative interactions, a 12:1 ratio is often used for self-esteem to counter the brain's innate negativity bias Try counting how many times you affirm your loved ones in your life.

We have an epidemic of "shoulding on ourselves" and it is time to clean that up (maybe with some of that fragrant toilet paper we are grateful for) and give ourselves some grace.

DO UNTO OTHERS

There is a reason why the Golden Rule (Matthew 7:12) says "Do to others what you would like them to do to you", is so important. God knew that if we treated others like we would like to be treated it would help us all.

In fact, other studies show that when we compliment or rejoice with another's accomplishments it kicks off a different chemical cocktail that can have an even more positive impact than just self-affirmation. In comparison, being a jerk is a toxic addition to your brain chemistry.

In an article on Neurolaunch.com September 15, 2024 with tons of validating references on "The Psychology of Giving Compliments-The Science Behind Positive Affirmations" where they list the neurological benefits to both the people we are affirming and to us when we give compliments to others.

Here are a few quotes from their article;

"When we give or receive a compliment, several regions of our brain light up like a Christmas tree. The striatum, a part of the brain associated with reward processing, gets particularly excited. This is the same area that responds to other pleasurable experiences, like eating chocolate or winning money."

They go on to say "But it's not just about pleasure. The medial prefrontal cortex, which plays a role in self-referential thinking, also gets involved. This suggests that compliments don't just make us feel good; they actually influence how we think about ourselves."

Some of the other neurotransmitter benefits that they talk about in their article as indicated by the research articles they site show that there is:

1. Dopamine Release: When we offer a compliment, it can trigger the release of dopamine in our brain. Dopamine is the "feel-good" neurotransmitter associated with feelings of pleasure and reward. This can enhance our mood and make us feel happier.

2. Oxytocin Boost: Complimenting others can also stimulate the release of oxytocin, the "love hormone" or "cuddle chemical." Oxytocin plays a significant role in building trust, strengthening relationships, and boosting feelings of connection and empathy.

3. Reduction in Stress: Engaging in positive interactions, such as giving compliments, can help reduce stress levels. The

interactions lead to a decrease in cortisol, the stress hormone, promoting a sense of well-being and calmness.

4. Enhanced Social Bonding: Compliments can enhance social bonding by creating positive interactions and reinforcing mutual appreciation and respect. This, in turn, contributes to better mental health and a supportive social network.

5. Improved Self-Esteem: Giving compliments can also improve one's own self-esteem. By focusing on others' positive traits, we cultivate a mindset of appreciation which can reflect back on ourselves, boosting our self-worth and confidence.

In other words, being kind to others creates a chemical party of peace and joy in our brains that changes how our body feels and how well we function in life. Doesn't it make sense to do it? Check out this story and see if it's worth it.

Overall, the act of giving a compliment doesn't just make others feel appreciated, but it also has profound positive effects on our own brain chemistry and emotional well-being. Here is another success story that really "sparks joy" for me (the Marie Kondo word used to get your house neat and tidy.)

RESCUE STORY #12 – JANE, THE SCHOOL TEACHER /ADHD MOM

Jane was a 32-year-old woman who walked into my office one day, plopped into the chair, and declared, "My family thinks I'm crazy, and I feel like I'm going to lose my mind and get fired."

Now, I hear a lot of dramatic opening lines, but Jane was convinced she had a severe, incurable mental illness due to past trauma.

She felt miserable at work, constantly argued with her husband, and her kids were running the house like a pack of unsupervised raccoons.

She complained that she could never sit still, yet somehow, nothing ever seemed to get done.

Her mind was like a hyperactive ping-pong ball, and to top it off, her family had unofficially declared her a hopeless case.

I do something most counselors and coaches are told never to do: I make promises.

Now, I can't change people, but I do promise that if someone applies the 3 G's the way I suggest, their mental state and life will change dramatically.

And let me tell you, Jane became my best proof of this system because she didn't just dip her toes in—she jumped right into it head first.

Jane was an educator, but she felt like she wasn't making much of a difference so she kept thinking she needed to find a more meaningful job.

Sure, her students were learning, but she figured they could do that with anyone and there must be some other place that she would be more "valuable."

She was waiting for that "big moment" when God would finally do something amazing with her life. In the meantime she was "shoulding" on herself which made her feel terrible.

Meanwhile, she was in a constant battle with her husband, and her kids had more control of the house than she did. She was mean and negative, saying hurtful things that she knew made everyone feel bad.

Now, I'll explain how you can use the 3 G's in more detail later, but the first thing we needed to do was change Jane's mindset instead of looking at it like she was the main character in "Jane, the Lousy Mom, Wife and Teacher" reality show.

I had her start by making a Gratitude list—yes, including her husband who she had to think about what she really appreciated about him but she soon realized he did much more than she had given him credit for, like going to work every day and taking out the trash.

She also listed things she appreciated about her kids and her job, her home (that she had wanted to move out of for years) and everything else she could think of.

Next, I had her make a list of everything she was Good at, obviously for her it was the most challenging task.

Now, despite being a well-educated professional, Jane struggled to see her own strengths. So, I told her to outsource the job—ask her kids, husband, colleagues, and friends what they thought she was good at.

The results were overwhelming (in a good way). Jane was not expecting to get 12 positive reinforcement statements for every negative thought she had, in fact she didn't expect any but she got them from everyone she asked. It changed her.

Finally, I had her set Goals—for her relationships, home, finances, job, and personal growth. The list was so long it could've doubled as a Dollar Tree receipt, but we broke it down into manageable pieces.

First up: the disaster zone she called home. Jane's house was an anxiety-inducing top of the line ADHD mess. Every time she walked in, she was greeted with piles of shoes, coats on the floor, papers covering the counters, and dishes stacked in a dangerous balancing act that could crash at any moment. It was enough to make anyone want to walk right back out the door.

Using the 3G's, we tackled the chaos. Jane started by telling herself: "I am Grateful for this home, and I am excited to make it beautiful and organized."

She reminded herself: "I'm Good at making a fresh start and organizing things when I put my mind to it."

Then, she set a Goal: "I will go to the store and get some bins and organizers to bring peace to my home."

Inspired by "Tidying Up with Marie Kondo", Jane got to work. She created designated spots for coats and shoes, labeled everything so her family couldn't pretend they didn't know where things belonged, and invested in pretty baskets to contain the clutter.

By the end of the day, she had accomplished more than she had in years.

Her kids, previously chaos specialists, were taught to use the 3 G's themselves. "I'm Grateful for my coat and shoes. I'm Good at putting things away. My Goal is to put my hat, coat and shoes away." Miraculously, they started following through.

As Jane continued applying the 3 G's at home and work, things changed. Her relationship with her husband improved dramatically. Instead of arguing, they communicated. Instead of feeling frustrated, they expressed appreciation. Her stress levels plummeted.

At work, she stopped waiting for a miraculous "calling" and realized she was already right where God wanted her. She began seeing her job as her mission field, not for preaching, but for leading by example.

She introduced the 3 G's to her students and colleagues, eventually even getting permission to present it to the staff. She became a go-to resource in her school, a beacon of positivity and change.

Now, Jane sees every moment of her life as part of her mission, a chance to help others transform just like she did. She is now working on completing her Phd, which she had never thought of before, and all it took was a little Gratitude, recognizing what she was Good at, and setting Goals, one step at a time.

So, if Jane could turn her life from an overwhelming mess into a thriving success story, what's stopping you?

FOOD FOR THOUGHT

1. Who is the last person that you said "you should" to and what was it about?

2. Do you have a hard time giving yourself compliments? If so why?

3. When you think about giving 12 positives for every negative where do you need to start?

4. How did Janes transformation make you feel? Are you ready to make changes?

JOURNALING THE 3 G'S AND MORE

BE A PERSPECTIVE SHIFTER

CHAPTER 12:

PERSPECTIVE SHIFTING ON STEROIDS

Life is hard. There are many people who don't fit in, who don't have opportunities, who have systemic disadvantages. who are simply different. Depending how we grew up, we may be looked at, or we may look at others as "not good enough" or "not fitting in." We call this "marginalized."

Many of us (myself included) are familiar with living in a situation with limited access to opportunities, resources and education. These things can be based on various factors including race, ethnicity, gender, sexual orientation, disability, age, and socioeconomic status.

For me, we were farmers in the 1950's and I am grateful to have learned to live on what we grew on the farm, hard work (whether you felt like it or not) and 2nd hand clothes, but going to college or joining the military was nothing my guidance counselor or anyone else talked about.

All three of my older brothers were drafted for the Vietnam war and besides getting married at 18, I didn't think I was smart enough to go to college.

I didn't know I had a legitimate reason that led to my less than great academic scores (ADHD) and I had no idea that women could go into the military, plus why would I want to risk being sent to VietNam?

Eventually I was given opportunities, government financial help and a desire to make changes in my life. I was also diagnosed with ADHD and started taking medication that really helped.

Another crucial thing was that my career counselor, Barb Webster, believed in me and convinced me I wasn't stupid and I had a lot to offer. She got me signed up at UW Superior through the extended degree program because I was a single mom, working part time and simply couldn't take the time to sit in a classroom.

I took my first class and got an A. I took another class and got an A. I decided maybe I wasn't as stupid as I had been led to believe so I went on to get my undergraduate and graduate degrees in counseling with a 3.67 GPA which is like an A- average.

WE ARE NOT ALWAYS WHAT WE APPEAR TO BE

When I was a school counselor, I remember a student who had been in the cognitively disabled special education program and had been determined to have an IQ score of 70 or less along with other criteria.

He was a very quiet withdrawn and almost hollow young boy. He rarely spoke and did minimal work. There was no support from home so school was his only hope.

In junior high it was discovered that he was being sexually abused by numerous people in his home and he was immediately removed and placed in foster care. Within weeks he was smiling, interacting, doing his homework and actually passing tests.

At the beginning of the next school year he was retested and he no longer met criteria for the CD program. His IQ had increased 15 points because he was in a safe place where he was not living with trauma every day.

His neural pathways were being healed and the muddy ruts of abuse were "drying up" (my non-scientific analogy) as he was free to go a different direction and he was creating a new neural pathway that focused on something more than merely surviving.

PERSPECTIVES THROUGH BROKEN GLASS

Realizing that you are a valuable human being that has a purpose in life, even if you aren't like others is crucial. My niece, Stephani Kunkel wrote a book called "Perspective's Through Broken Glass-A Guide to Navigating Depression at Home and in The Workplace"

Stephanie's book is a great example of how someone can go from "Zero to Hero" as she began her journey depressed and suicidal and now is a highly sought after speaker, trainer and business and life coach.

Stephanie founded the organization "Perspective Shifters LLC" and now added "The Rebel DreamLab" to her network of business owners who all come from different backgrounds, beliefs and often, traumatic experiences like Stephanie has.

It was through these challenges and the uphill battle of entrepreneurship that these men and women found their way out of a less than joy-filled life to living their purpose with joy and anticipation.

This is what it is all about. If we could only find the good in our lives, in one another, and the world in general we would be much happier. We are meant to do this life together because we are all differently abled and can offer great services to one another (Stephanie has been my business coach for over a year now and she is awesome.)

It's OK to admit we need help and that someone who is 30 years younger (like my niece) just may be more skilled to accomplish something that may take us 20 times longer if we ever get it done at all! It only requires us to shift our perspective and humble ourselves enough to be ok with not being able to do everything all of the time.

My favorite memory of my life as a Career Counselor for the Wisconsin Department of Workforce Development that was probably the epitome of perspective shifting was Toby, a referral from the Marathon County Jail. Be sure to read the next chapter to get an amazing success story and a good laugh.

FOOD FOR THOUGHT

1. What are some things that you need to start looking at from a different perspective?

___

___

___

2. What "broken glass" do you have in your life story that has caused problems in your view of yourself and/or others?

___

___

___

3. What changes can you make to move forward in life

___

___

___

4. Who can you reach out to or what can you do to get the "coaching" and support you need to help you shift your perspective?

___

___

___

JOURNALING THE 3 G'S AND MORE

___

___

___

___

___

___

___

___

___

THINGS ARE NOT ALWAYS AS THEY APPEAR LOOK FOR THE GOOD

RESCUE STORY #13 – TOBY, TRANSFERABLE SKILLS OF THE PROFESSIONAL DRUG DEALER

It was spring of 1999 when I got a call from the jail in my hometown. I was the career counselor for the Job Center and the transition assistant was having a really hard time helping Toby to get a job and she knew I had a knack for doing resumes of challenging clients.

Toby was released from jail to come and meet with me. He was a tall well built black man who presented somewhat shy and reserved. He was very discouraged because he had been looking for a job for 6 months and had not even had one response.

He had a couple of challenges. First, he was in jail with a drug charge. Second, he was not from our town and he was not white. There were very few black people in our town except for the Hmong refugees. Those who were here were only featured in our community paper when they ended up in jail so employers had little experience which meant that they were not the first people to be chosen for a job.

I asked Toby to tell me about his work history. He was almost 25 and was from a large city in Southern Wisconsin so I expected at least he had food service experience but nope. Nada. Never worked. Anywhere!

Fortunately, I was raised to believe that everyone was created with special gifts, talents and abilities that no one else in the world ever has had or ever will have because none of us are alike.

The challenge was to help Toby and other people like him discover the good they have to offer and how to get paid to do it in a legitimate lifestyle. I asked Toby what kind of job he might consider and he said he was interested in customer service or manufacturing so this is the resume we came up with;

TRANSFERABLE SKILLS

1. CUSTOMER SERVICE AND SALES – Able to develop a satisfied and loyal customer base by identifying, anticipating, and providing products at a reasonable cost in a timely manner.

2. PURCHASING AND DELIVERY – Able to identify high-quality, low-cost product suppliers and set up safe, reliable, and prompt delivery methods while maintaining a high-profit margin.
3. PERSONNEL MANAGEMENT – Interviewed, hired, trained, and supervised dependable, honest, and trustworthy staff ensuring that outlets in several cities were operating with positive results.
4. FINANCIAL MANAGEMENT – Built a successful business from the ground up by establishing tight inventory control, requiring up-front payment for products, promptly collecting any outstanding debts and successfully establishing and managing budgets.
5. MANUFACTURING – Experienced in receiving raw materials. setting up a manufacturing product line, filling product orders to specification, packaging and shipping products in a timely manner.

COME ON NOW, what are you laughing at?? I realize many think this is a dishonest way for a drug dealer to present themselves. But, to run a successful business for 10 years without getting arrested or ending up dead, clearly, he had all the skills listed right??

After six months of looking for a job without as much as one call back, he got a job in customer service in only a week with this new strategy! Granted it wasn't on the resume alone because he had some explaining to do, like why he was in jail and why his only references were the jailer and his probation officer!

Writing a letter of introduction/intent is a must in this job market so we had to write one. Now I don't recommend this approach for probably 95% of my job seekers but we didn't have much to lose.

The cover letter was a simple "I have screwed up my life and made a lot of bad choices but I really do have the skills listed on my resume and I am ready to live an honest life."

Ok... you know that is not exactly how I worded it but you get the idea right?

We also had to practice interviewing because when you don't think you have anything to offer and you are used to talking about yourself in negative terms it is a chance to be positive and confident. You may need to write it down and practice.

He called me nine years after he got that first job to tell me he had moved from his customer service job to take a job in manufacturing where he had been working for over eight years.

He had never been in trouble again, but without a different approach, he may have been "stuck" in a drug dealer lifestyle because that is all he had believed he could do.

Self-esteem grows from self-appreciation and taking time to reflect on what you like about yourself. I helped Toby to realize that he had many things he was Good at, that he could be Grateful for the opportunity to get a job and he had a Goal to get and keep a job and stay sober in the process.

The 3 G's transformed his life and gave him HOPE for the future.

FOOD FOR THOUGHT

1. Have you ever had the attitude of "those people" that you were judgmental about? Who? What were you thinking?

2. Why is this thinking not helpful for having a good world that works together?

3. Have you ever had anyone judge you in a way that wasn't who you were?

4. Think of one person that you have judged and determined to know the other side of them. Who would that be and how could you find the good in them?

JOURNALING THE 3 G'S AND MORE

CHAPTER 13:

CREATED BY GOD FOR RIGHT HERE, RIGHT NOW

RESCUE STORY – #14 MARY, THE STAY AT HOME MOM

Mary was in her late 50's when she arrived at the Job Center in desperation. Her husband had passed and she had never worked and had no retirement to fall back on.

Mary still had kids living at home to support but she said to me "I have no skills and have never looked for a job or done a resume. I don't have anything to put on it because I really have never done anything.

Now Mary had six children and had homeschooled all of them. Two of the children were in college and two others had already graduated and were in successful careers. The youngest two were still at home.

It doesn't take a rocket scientist to see all the things that Mary was Good at, nor does it take a rocket scientist to reach her Goal of getting a job. It only took a little self introspection, confidence and creativity to catapult this powerhouse of a woman into the workplace.

Like Toby, Mary had demonstrated skills that every employer prays for (well maybe they don't all pray but you may hear them let out a lingo of frustration asking God to damn the person who doesn't show up for work…again!)

Mary was Grateful for this opportunity and being able to see what she had to offer. She showed up, every day, all day, for her husband and 6 kids. Her resume looked like this

- Child Development & Education:
    - Homeschooled six children from kindergarten through high school, ensuring academic achievement and personal development by adapting teaching methods to individual learning styles and developmental needs.
- Budgeting & Financial Management:
    - Managed household budget, tracked expenses, and optimized purchases to ensure financial stability and savings.
- Cooking & Meal Planning:
    - Planned and prepared nutritious meals that cater to diverse dietary needs and preferences
- Time Management & Organization:
    - Efficiently balanced multiple responsibilities, appointments, and activities to ensure smooth daily operations.
- Problem Solving & Adaptability:
    - Developed creative solutions to everyday challenges and adapted to changing needs and dynamics.
- Communication & Interpersonal Skills:
    - Facilitated open and effective communication within the household and external community networks.

EXPERIENCE

1978-1999-Domestic Engineer, Manager & Educator for last 28 years.

Community Volunteer at St. Vincent De Paul's Homeless Program and Thrift Store

Mary was in tears as she realized that she really did have something to offer others. It did not take her long to find a rewarding career in the educational system as a teacher's aide using this skills format resume and a cover letter highlighting who she was as a person and what she had to offer.

PROOF YOU HAVE MORE TO OFFER

Some people have a hard time acknowledging their giftedness because they equate their value on the world's definition of success which usually is about money.

I was fortunate enough to be led to these following verses 49 years ago that helped me to realize that not only did God create me to be an amazing human, but he also gave me the talents and ability to use my giftedness to transform lives. "The Spirit of God has made me; the breath of the Almighty gives me life." Job 33:4

These Bible verses highlight being created by God, emphasizing His craftsmanship, intentionality, and purpose in creating each and every one of us:

- **Genesis 1:27**
  "So God created man in his own image, in the image of God he created him; male and female he created them."
- **Psalm 139:13-14**
  "For you created my inmost being; you knit me together in my mother's womb. I praise you because I am fearfully and wonderfully made; your works are wonderful, I know that full well."
- **Isaiah 64:8**
  "Yet you, Lord, are our Father. We are the clay, you are the potter; we are all the work of your hand."
- **Ephesians 2:10**
  "For we are God's handiwork, created in Christ Jesus to do good works, which God prepared in advance for us to do."

- **Isaiah 43:7**
  "Everyone who is called by my name, whom I created for my glory, whom I formed and made."

In other words, God created us just the way he wanted us and then he gave us amazing gifts, talents, experiences and interests to share with each other so we can all be our best together.

Here are some of the different spiritual gifts the Bible talks about that God has given us. (There are more but we will focus on these for now.)

1. Service: The ability to willingly aid and serve others.
2. Teaching: The gift of explaining and applying Biblical truths effectively.
3. Exhortation: Encouraging and motivating others toward growth and action.
4. Giving: The ability to share resources generously.
5. Leadership: Guiding and managing others well, with wisdom and Godliness.
6. Mercy: Demonstrating compassion and empathy toward those who are suffering.

Can you imagine how awesome it would be if at minimum, those of us who call ourselves Christians actually followed this! Even the title of this next passage in the New International Version should give many of us a slap upside the head! (I call it a God slap...LOL.)

UNITY AND DIVERSITY IN THE BODY

Remember when I talked about being a Faucet of HOPE? The whole point of that is letting the spirit flow through us to share our gifts and talents with others and that that's the spirit that he's talking about in that verse. On to the next verses in chapter 12...

I Corinthians 12:12 "For just as the body is one and has many members, and all the members of the body, though many, are one body, so it is with Christ."

13 For in one Spirit we were all baptized into one body—Jews or Greeks, slaves[d] or free—and all were made to drink of one Spirit.

14 For the body does not consist of one member but of many.

I Corinthians 12:15 "Now if the foot should say, "Because I am not a hand, I do not belong to the body," it would not for that reason stop being part of the body."

16 And if the ear should say, "Because I am not an eye, I do not belong to the body," it would not for that reason stop being part of the body.

17 If the whole body were an eye, where would the sense of hearing be? If the whole body were an ear, where would the sense of smell be?

18 But as it is, God arranged the members in the body, each one of them, as he chose.

19 If all were a single member, where would the body be?

20 As it is, there are many parts, yet one body.

21 The eye cannot say to the hand, "I have no need of you," nor again the head to the feet, "I have no need of you."

22 On the contrary, the parts of the body that seem to be weaker are indispensable,

23 and on those parts of the body that we think less honorable we bestow the greater honor, and our unpresentable parts are treated with greater modesty.

24 which our more presentable parts do not require. But God has so composed the body, giving greater honor to the part that lacked it,

25 that there may be no division in the body, but that the members may
have the same care for one another. 26 If one member suffers, all suffer
together; if one member is honored, all rejoice together.

I DIGRESS– I know that was a huge paragraph but did you ever wonder why someone thought that plopping a new verse number in the middle of a sentence was a great idea? Clearly they did not have Miss Lucas for an English teacher and I couldn't figure out how to break up the paragraph!

Now that I have you off track going back to assess that big paragraph and the logic of splitting those verses, I will ask you to come on back and let's move on… LOL!

Those verses should give all of us reason to pause and look at those who have been looked at as hopeless, and not worth giving another thought to, or offering a job or having a relationship with.

When I was a career counselor, I tried to convince employers that many of the ex-offenders and disabled people may be their greatest irreplaceable assets if they only look for the value.

It always upsets me to hear an employer threaten a worker with "if you don't like it then just leave!" They would say "there's always another person waiting for the job."

We were simply not trained in our society to look for the good in people and bring it out. We don't seem to know how to empower them to see how valuable they really are but if we did, we would find they often step up and do a lot more than we even hope.

Can you imagine how different life would be if we honored the janitor, and volunteers as much as we honored the pastor and CEO?

Or what if we all suffered along with the homeless, the hungry, the orphan, the widow, the sick and those in prison rather than treating them like they are worthless or too much of a burden or don't deserve to be bothered with.

Be a Faucet of HOPE
HOPE: Help, Opportunity, Praise and Encouragement

We are ALL created to be irreplaceable assets in the world yet as hard as I tried to get employers to see that if they could simply give that ex-offender, that person without a high school diploma, the homeless, or the blind or deaf person a chance, they would discover the most valuable employee they ever had. Unfortunately very few made that choice.

How about you? Are you ready to start looking at yourself and others as God created gifts to change the world? If so, keep talking to yourself and everyone else! Your brain is going to love you for it and so will everyone else.

FOOD FOR THOUGHT

1. What are some areas that would be helpful for you to use your gifts to help others?

   ____

   ____

   ____

2. Why do you feel you are an irreplaceable asset to the world?

   ____

   ____

   ____

3. Who are the people that you could be more accepting toward?

   ____

   ____

   ____

4. What could you do to help our world be a better place?

   ____

   ____

   ____

JOURNALING - YOU CAN PRACTICE YOUR 3 G'S OR WRITE ANYTHING ELSE HERE AS YOU FEEL LED

PART IV

GO OUT AND LIVE SUCCESSFULLY GOALS

CHAPTER 14

THE CHALLENGE AND POWER OF GOALS

In this chapter we are going to go deeper into how goals impact the brain, body and spirit. The main reason people come to me as a counselor or a life coach is to reach goals.

Most often the goals are to lose weight, quit drinking, communicate better, be less anxious or depressed, make decisions etc.

As a counselor. I have to document the success of treatment by getting a baseline to how someone is feeling about themselves and then track to see if my treatment methodology is helping at all to improve their goals.

Like I said, in the first chapter, I can't change anyone, but I guarantee that if they use the 3 G's "as prescribed" it will make significant changes in their lives and the lives of those they come in contact with because it is scientifically and statistically proven.

For every client I work with, the first goal I give them as part of their treatment plan is to have the goal of doing the 3 G's list of everything they can think of that they are grateful for, everything they can think of that they are good at, and everything they can think of that they are wanting to accomplish.

To be honest, very few people get that done in the first week and if they do it at all, the lists are probably very short because they're just not used to this change in perspective to write down EVERYTHING. We just don't think about it.

Frankly, most of us aren't used to using our brains much at all when it comes to mindfulness so we just float through the day willy-nilly as though we haven't even shifted our brains into gear to be aware of what's going on around us.

The other thing is that these lists will change daily as we become more mindful of the things that matter in life and who we are and what we're doing and what we want to do.

For me, my goals have to start with asking God to speak to me and give me a direction because left to my own devices, I will do whatever feels good at the moment (binge watching TV with a bag of chips) but I believe God has a plan for us every day which is better than my mindless choices. The only way to find out what that purpose is, is to ask him.

If you don't already have my book *Speak to Me God I'm Listening-365 Daily Meditations For Those Who Want to Hear God Answer Life's Toughest Questions,* this would be a good time to get it because in the beginning I go through how to go about praying for God's will and how to listen for the answer.

For many people, they go to God to get direction, but they have no idea how to be quiet long enough to listen and hear him speak to them after they pray. I believe that if we could make that spiritual connection, and begin to follow that divine guidance, it would change the world!

I know there are a lot of people that are reading this book that aren't "religious" or do not claim to be "Christian" but you know what? – It doesn't matter. This is a no judgment area and if you are still reading after all the Bible stuff I have shared, that shows me you are open to spiritual guidance.

I know I have mentioned this before, but when people ask me how I know that God is real and that the Bible is true, and that Jesus is worth serving, I have to tell them that I do not have unequivocal proof of any of it, but I believe it because He made himself real to me in 1976, I didn't kill myself like I was going to, and the peace I experience with Him every day transcends any earthly peace I ever had without Him.

I can't explain it all, but I choose to believe it and that's all that really matters. Just like you reading this book; you can choose to believe what I say in it, or not. It is entirely up to you.

All I know is that I have given God (as I understand Him) the true test of time (71 years) and he has proven himself over and over again. I believe he will do the same with you and will also show you that the 3 G's is a solid methodology that will work because he came up with the idea to begin with and I'm just sharing it (with His permission of course.)

RESCUE STORY – #15 JACK, THE MARINE LANDSCAPING AND LAWN CARE

Jack was another veteran who joined our program after getting his third drunk driving and facing several months in jail. He was very depressed and ashamed.

Jack had been on a variety of jobs but his passion and primary goal was to own his own business but he wasn't sure what he wanted to do but he had procrastinated because it was stressful to think about it so he drank instead.

Jack joined our rehabilitation program which offered a wide variety of opportunities including being trained in our secondhand store, lawn care, snow removal, small engine repair, repairing furniture, customer service and sales, bookkeeping, marketing and many other things, including operating a food truck.

Jack really gravitated toward outdoor work and quickly took the lead in the lawn care business. He received a lot of recommendations from our customers and they regularly requested him to do their lawn care and snow removal.

When Jack had fulfilled his probation time with the department of corrections and got his license back, he started his own landscaping and snow removal business and grew to the point where he needed to hire staff.

Jack was a marine and did not like asking for help so it was really hard for him to come into this program, but he learned that he could be grateful for the opportunity to be in our program so he could get a start doing what he's always wanted to do but never had the support to do it.

He didn't even know he had the ability to do everything that was needed to run a business, but he allowed us to help him and he followed his goals using the 3 G's to keep him motivated, confident and grateful each step of the way.

Jack was given HOPE to move forward and he used his circumstances to make a fresh start. He was an example of Romans 8:28 where it says "God works all things together for the good for those who love God and are called according to His purposes."

We can be that HOPE to others... it is part of our purpose. Are you ready to offer HOPE to others? Are you willing to ask for it when you need it?

LESS MESS = MORE FOCUS

MORE FOCUS = LESS MESS

GOAL SETTING IS HARD

For many of us, setting goals is overwhelming because we think we've got to have things scheduled for the next 50 years or something, but that's not the case.

For me, I pray in the morning for God to give me some direction of what needs to be done for the day.

Then I go to my "speaktomegodimlistening" Facebook page and I add my 3 G's to our twice a day posts so I can be accountable to others for things I want to accomplish. I also want to be an example to them of a consistent commitment to something that helps us in our lives.

For some people getting out of the bed may be their first goal in the morning because that's a really hard thing to do for those that are depressed, in pain, or simply too tired to try.

If you take one minute at a time like I had to when I quit drinking, it will give you a whole lot more dopamine because you are kicking those chemicals off in your brain every minute you are cheering yourself on to success all day long.

For example, I use it when I'm doing my laundry which is a real challenge for many of us ADHDer's. I see some of you nodding out there in camaraderie with me!

I also see many of you irritated housemates (like my husband and all the housemates I have had over the years) who live with an ADHDer as you have watched them struggle to get the clothes off the floor, into the hamper, then to the washer, dryer and back into the closet in a timely way.

So here is what I do... I pump myself up by saying I am Grateful that I have clothes to wash and a washer and dryer to use to wash them with and my Goal is to go to the basement and put them in the washer.

I cheer myself on with- "I am Good at getting my load of laundry going and I'm Grateful that I have soap and water to wash them with. Yay! Great job Linda!

Now I set a new goal by setting my alarm for as long as my washing machine takes. When the alarm goes off I say "yay…clothes are done, I am going to go right away and put them in the dryer" with the same verbal routine.

I continue that pattern until I get them all the way back up into my closet hung up, color-coded (because that sparks joy for me) and put in my drawer organizers. I give myself kudos every step of the way.

You can do this with every single goal as well, but you need to be mindful and make choices many many times a day.

Why make such a big deal out of goals? Because goals are the foundation of everything. Maybe this should've gone first in the book because doing your gratitude list is a goal.

Telling yourself you're good at something is a goal but for me, if I don't wake up in the morning with my first thing being gratitude, and I try to make setting goals the first thing, I would be overwhelmed with my to do list. I have to connect with God first, and I do that through gratitude.

Why does this work so well? It goes back to our addictive nature of wanting that dopamine hit that feels good and accomplishing goals feels good! In fact, procrastinating on it can make you sick and fat!

What? Yes, you heard me right. Procrastination causes increased cortisol, the body's primary stress hormone. Delaying tasks leads to chronic stress, guilt, and anxiety, which triggers the brain to release cortisol and adrenaline.

This creates a vicious cycle where chronic procrastination raises stress levels, leading to further procrastination and weight gain and many other negative things.

Unfortunately sitting on the couch eating chips also sparks dopamine which is motivating…at the moment! We have to really think about the goal setting process and figure out why we are setting goals to begin with and then consider how to kick the chemistry into gear so we feel good about reaching them.

PROCRASTINATION: THE SNACK-SIZE STRESSOR THAT TURNS INTO FULL-SIZE CORTISOL AND PLUS SIZE CLOTHES!

FOOD FOR THOUGHT

1. What are some of your top goals that you have been putting off that you would like to accomplish?

2. Why do you feel you haven't reached them yet?

3. What strategies could you use to be more successful?

4. Who could you ask for help?

JOURNALING THE 3 G'S AND MORE

CHAPTER 15:

THE SCIENCE OF GOALS

WHY YOUR BRAIN IS BOTH AN ANGEL AND A DEVIL

I find this scientific stuff fascinating and I wish I could remember all the terms off the top of my 71 year old ADHD/ hypo-mania Type II brain when I am sharing about it, but our brains are complicated!

I (and my parents, co-workers, teachers and family) have found that memorizing stuff, even cool, important stuff, has never been my strong suit.

It is also hard to explain all of this mumbo jumbo so once again I am giving you even more analogous images for you to ponder and try to tuck away in your own thoughts for future reference.

WARNING – If you are being quizzed in your college medical terminology class, describing the prefrontal cortex as your inner CEO or life coach or talking about cheerleaders and gremlins, or angels and devils as your brain chemistry descriptions probably won't get you the grade you are looking for!

Many of these brain parts and chemicals are the same ones we have already talked about, but I was thinking a little different view might help to lock it in the brain!

Here is what goal setting does for us , , ,

1. THE PREFRONTAL CORTEX – YOUR INNER LIFE COACH

In the first chapter I called this "your ultimate life coach" but you could also consider it your inner CEO, boss…or perhaps the spirit or again like mom said…the angel on one shoulder.

This is the part of your brain that makes plans, sets priorities, and tries to keep you from making terrible decisions.

It helps you "play it to the end" at least it will try to if you are willing to listen to things like…

"If I go to the gym, I'll feel great later."

Unfortunately, it also gets tired when you have taxed it too much through physical or mental work and it loses the ability to help you focus, make good decisions and your intentions to work out could turn into the protective supportive, take time for yourself life coach (who may be enabling at times) that may say something like…

"Hey, I get you are tired, so instead of going to the gym maybe you need to take some time and watch Netflix for four hours and eat nachos."

Clearly between this and the next brain function it is imperative we use conscious mindfulness to direct our thoughts and attention!

2. THE VENTRAL STRIATUM – THE DOPAMINE DEALER

This is, in my opinion, the part of our brain that is foundational to goal setting and achieving because it is literally the drug dealer of our brains that kicks off chemicals that give us that "feel good rush" that keeps us motivated and inspired to do both good stuff and bad…depending on what motivates us.

It includes the Nucleus Accumbens (NAc) which receives the chemicals from the Ventral Striatum and then motivates you to go ahead and do what feels good.

Tell me, do you ever get a little rush from checking something off your to-do list? That's dopamine.

- You resist a temptation → dopamine hit!
- You do a surprise party for a loved one and they are thrilled → dopamine hit!
- You eat a healthy meal instead of junk food → dopamine hit!
- You get a huge bonus at work for doing well → big dopamine hit!

The trick? Set small, achievable steps so you keep getting healthy rewards along the way. Like if you decided not to go to the gym, at least get up and walk around during every commercial so you can get those little dopamine hits every 10 minutes.

Keep in mind that if we are not working on mindfulness, this little brain part can trick us into getting the dopamine from alcohol, drugs, chocolate or lots of other things that aren't so good for us. You decide which one to listen to.

3. THE AMYGDALA – THE DRAMA QUEEN

This little almond-shaped part of your brain runs on emotions and decides what's worth getting excited about or freaking out over.

If you've ever abandoned a goal the second things got hard, blame your amygdala. It wants to keep you "safe" even if that means clinging to bad habits.

So how does the Queen work?

- You start the day by setting a goal? Exciting!
- Face a setback? The world is ending!
- Thought about doing something risky? Fight-or-flight mode engaged!
- Emotions kick in and you fly into old patterns unless you are mindful and the anterior cingulate cortex kicks in.

4. THE ANTERIOR CINGULATE CORTEX ACC – YOUR GPS/INNER CRITIC

The ACC is located in the front of your brain between the two hemispheres like someone who chose the perfect seat to watch all the emotional and cognitive drama unfold when you are trying to get to your destination. It is close enough to both the thinking and the feeling parts to be yelling at both!

- Your GPS tells you to get up and go meet your friend at the gym at 7 a.m. and you get up but then the phone dings and you think it might be your friend.
- You quickly hit the message only to find it is a tik tok video from a friend that you decide you will watch real quick that sends you on a 20 minute tangent until you hear the inner critic say "hey what are you doing? Stop that- you are late to the gym" and then the GPS kicks in to say "rerouting".
- Next thing you know the emotional part of the ACC kicks in and you are on the Fight-or-flight mode which is now engaged! OMG what will my friend say...she will be so mad. I will only have ½ hour to work out. I was so stupid.
- Emotions kick in and you fly into old patterns UNLESS you are mindful and not get offended by the inner critic trying to help you get back on track and not guilt trip you for needing to reboot.

IN SUMMARY: THE ACC HELPS WITH

- Error detection ("That was a mistake")
- Pain and emotional distress ("Ouch, that hurt... but you will get through it")
- Motivation and effort ("Do we really have to?")
- Attention and control ("Focus, please")

- Emotional regulation ("They might be upset but let's not cry in the gym")

I find it fascinating how these brain activities change the brain chemistry that changes the body's response to everything we eat, hear, think, taste, feel, smell and do.

ABOUT THOSE CHEMICAL COCKTAILS

In the past, I've talked about chemicals, not just the ones that come from what we eat and drink, but the ones our brains create from what we think. Yes: your mind is not a passenger. It's a factory."

Dr. Anna Lembke, Stanford's addiction, psychiatrist describes a fascinating process related to addiction in her book "Dopamine Nation: Finding Balance in the Age of Indulgence. 2023" called the Gremlin Theory. The brain, she explains, doesn't just chase pleasure—it also tries to correct for it.

I am going to try to explain it using my own metaphor, which is a little different, but you will get the concept. Check hers out anyway. It's fascinating.

"Here's the challenge: your brain treats pleasure and pain like they're on the same internal control panel. When something floods your system with pleasure (and dopamine), your brain doesn't say, 'Great! Let's stay like this forever. Instead, it moves in to restore balance, like a thermostat that can't stand the room being too hot for too long.

Think of it like this:

The Angel wants calm, steady energy. It wants you to feel okay in a normal, grounded way, more steady than spinning.

The Devil wants relief right now. It whispers that you need more, one more hit, one more drink, one more scroll, one more escape, because it's trying to turn down uncomfortable feelings fast.

Comedown/withdrawal = your brain sends out a warning when you repeatedly try to chase pleasure and the angel gets bigger to tip the scale back to normal but because coming off the overindulgence you get cravings, irritability, restlessness, 'I don't feel right unless I do it again. It's not just willpower, it's your brain trying to rebalance.

Tolerance/addiction = devil starts to run the show and with repeated, excessive exposure, the devil doesn't just return, it accumulates. Eventually, what you used to do for enjoyment turns into something you do just to feel normal. The goal quietly changes from "I want to feel high" to "I need to counteract the devil so I can stop feeling awful."

Homeostasis = angel brings you back to center. Now the hopeful part: when you stop feeding the pleasure-delivery system, whether it's a substance or a behavior, the devil slowly loses its power. Over time, abstinence helps the brain's balance settle back into something calmer.

Homeostasis isn't instant, but it is real: your baseline mood and your ability to cope gradually return but Dr. Lembke and other researchers state it takes about 30 days of abstinence for your brain to get back to balanced.

So the question isn't only "How do I avoid temptation?" It's also: "How do I help my angel prevent and help me re-learn balance so my devil stops driving the steering wheel?"

And all this is going on and we are in la la land wondering why we are not doing well! And there is more!

Here are the chemicals that are produced when we go through the process of trying to find balance between pain and pleasure.

- Dopamine is that best friend chemical everyone wants to hang out with: As you set goals and make progress, little bursts of dopamine are released, giving you that "Oh yeah, I can do this!" feeling.
- Endorphins are like your olympic training, coach chemical: These feel-good chemicals help reduce pain and increase pleasure. They are the ones at the last 100 yards cheering you on to hit the finish line.

- Serotonin, the social butterfly: This brain chemical really comes out when you're feeling proud of an achievement. Serotonin likes to keep the peace and liven the mood, making everyone feel connected and jovial. It's like that friend who makes sure everyone's having a good time and feeling valued.
- Oxytocin, the gentle hugger: This might show up when you're celebrating a success with others. Oxytocin is all about bonding and trust. It's like when someone gives you a big warm hug for setting and achieving your goals, whispering, "You're amazing!"

You can see how alcohol, food, drugs, gambling, scrolling the internet, gaming or even working can give you reinforcing chemicals that keep us feeling good.

The problem with all this feel good activity and achievement chemical partying, is that some of us are way too indulgent and end up "hungover" and/or burned out.

Yes, the fact is, you can even get addicted to things like work by constantly doing, doing, doing, things with no balance. They call it workaholism, so be careful.

But if you think about it, isn't it better to catch the bug of being an accomplished goal setter for things you know spark joy than to sit in the shame of purposeless procrastination scrolling Tik Tok, eating potato chips and getting drunk?

If you want to reach your goals, listen to the angel's voice and stop using the devil's excuse "I don't feel like it"

BE A ONE MINUTE MANAGER

I was a career counselor for 15 years and I learned a lot about why people ended up in the job center looking for work. Some of them had been laid off, but a large number of them had either quit or gotten fired because they had personality conflicts on the job or they weren't motivated enough to do the job.

When employers began using the 3 G's it changed everything. One of the best books I have read for business is *The One Minute Manager* by Ken Blanchard and Spencer Johnson. It is a short, practical book that introduces a straightforward approach to effective management and it coincides with the 3 G's Method beautifully.

The book centers on three "One Minute" techniques aimed at helping managers lead more efficiently while fostering positive relationships with their team members. Here's a summary of the main ideas:

1. **One Minute Goals:** The idea is to set clear, concise goals that can be read in one minute. Both the manager and the employee understand and agree on what's expected, which aligns everyone's focus. This clarity prevents misunderstandings and helps employees stay on track.

2. **One Minute Praisings:** Managers take a moment to give immediate, specific, and sincere praise to employees when they do something well. This boosts morale, reinforces desired behaviors, and builds confidence.

3. **One Minute Reprimands:** When things don't go as expected, the manager provides quick, constructive feedback. They point out what went wrong, explain why it matters, and then reassure the employee, emphasizing that it's their performance, not them as a person, that's being addressed.

These techniques are designed to be simple but effective, improving communication, boosting productivity, and creating a positive work environment.

The 3 G's take it a step further in that people learn to do that for themselves so they're not depending on external motivation, but they are giving themselves praise and reprimand and goalsetting, and discovering their own purpose.

I've been doing corporate training for well over 30 years to help businesses create a more mental health friendly workplace. Studies are very clear that when a workplace is sensitive to the mental health needs of their employees and families they will have better retention, increased productivity, better attendance and greater job satisfaction.

When I teach the 3 G's, the One Minute Manager and healthy supportive communication, people learn that they simply feel better about themselves, their co-workers, their families and their lives. They are able to see the good in others and can see how collaborating and cooperating as a team makes everyone feel better and get more accomplished.

Can you imagine how helpful it would be if your manager came in each morning and told you one thing they were Grateful for that you did at work, one thing you were Good at and discuss one Goal that you have reached that helped the company accomplish?

It would be a lot easier to hear them share the bumps in the road you have encountered as they offered their help to get you back on the right track. Employees rarely get that kind of support.

I am sure employers would say they rarely get that kind of encouragement from their employees either, so why not be the first one to do that? (Maybe leave off the one minute reprimand just to be safe!)

PAY IT FORWARD

GIVING TO OTHERS CHANGES YOU

Have you ever watched the movie "Pay it Forward?" If not, you need to. You will see that when a society leans in to paying it forward the whole world can be transformed.

I experience this whenever I go to an Aldi food store and have to pay a quarter to get a cart which is given back to you when you return the cart. If you have ever gone shopping and not had a quarter it is a real pain to shop without a cart.

My simple gesture to help others who may have this problem is to give people my cart when I am done so they don't have to dig for a quarter. I simply ask them to pay it forward. You would think that I was giving them $100!

People are so grateful for this small kind gesture that they are more than happy to pay it forward. Why? Because paying it forward feels good as it taps into a powerful combination of emotional, social, and even physiological benefits. Here's what the research shows that paying it forward does for us:

1. Sense of Purpose and Meaning: Acts of kindness can provide a feeling of purpose. When you pay it forward, you're contributing to something bigger than yourself, which can add a layer of fulfillment to your life.

2. Release of "Feel-Good" Chemicals: Kindness stimulates the production of dopamine and serotonin, which are the brain's natural mood boosters. It also promotes the release of oxytocin, known as the "love hormone," which can help you feel connected to others.

3. Building Social Connections: Paying it forward fosters a sense of connection with others. Even if you don't see the full impact, there's a feeling of shared goodwill that can remind you of the power of human connection.

4. Boosting Self-Esteem and Self-Worth: Helping others can make you feel more valuable and capable. This can lead to greater

confidence and self-worth, knowing that you have something positive to offer the world.

5. Creating a Positive Ripple Effect: Paying it forward often creates a chain reaction of kindness. Knowing that your actions may inspire others to do the same can lead to an uplifting sense of impact and legacy.
6. Breaking the Cycle of Stress and Anxiety: Focusing on someone else's well-being, even for a brief moment, can reduce stress by shifting your attention away from your own worries. The act itself can bring a sense of calm and reduce cortisol levels.

In short, helping others not only lifts them up, it boosts your own well-being, too. This is another goal that combines what we are Grateful for, what someone else is Good at and the Goal to change a life.

THOUGHTS CAUSE FEELINGS AND FEELINGS CAUSE BEHAVIORS

I have given you a bunch of my favorite one-liners but I have a lot more that have influenced me over the years that I thought I would share with you. I hope they help you as much as they have helped me.

1. "A goal without a plan is just a wish." – Antoine de Saint-Exupéry
2. "Setting goals is the first step in turning the invisible into the visible." – Tony Robbins
3. "You can't hit a target you cannot see, and you cannot see a target you do not have." – Zig Ziglar
4. "If you fail to plan, you are planning to fail." – Benjamin Franklin
5. "Discipline is the bridge between goals and accomplishment." – Jim Rohn
6. "What gets measured gets managed." – Peter Drucker
7. "A journey of a thousand miles begins with a single step." – Lao Tzu
8. "Goals are dreams with deadlines." – Napoleon Hill (often attributed)
9. "The tragedy in life doesn't lie in not reaching your goal. The tragedy lies in having no goal to reach." – Benjamin E. Mays
10. "You are never too old to set another goal or to dream a new dream." – C.S. Lewis
11. "Success is the progressive realization of a worthy ideal." – Earl Nightingale
12. "People with goals succeed because they know where they are going." – Earl Nightingale
13. "Begin with the end in mind." – Stephen R. Covey
14. "A goal properly set is halfway reached." – Zig Ziglar
15. "The future depends on what you do today." – Mahatma Gandhi

16. "Small daily improvements over time lead to stunning results." – Robin Sharma
17. "You miss 100% of the shots you don't take." – Wayne Gretzky
18. "You don't have to be great to start, but you have to start to be great." – Zig Ziglar
19. "Motivation gets you going, but discipline keeps you growing." – John C. Maxwell
20. "Success is the sum of small efforts, repeated day in and day out." – Robert Collier
21. "You do not rise to the level of your goals. You fall to the level of your systems." – James Clear
22. "Commit your work to the LORD, and your plans will be established." Proverbs 16:3
23. "Setting goals is the first step in turning the invisible into the visible." – Tony Robbins
24. "The plans of the diligent lead surely to abundance, but everyone who is hasty comes only to poverty." Proverbs 21:5
25. "Discipline is the bridge between goals and accomplishment." – Jim Rohn
26. "For I know the plans I have for you, declares the Lord, plans for welfare and not for evil, to give you a future and a hope." Jeremiah 29:11 (He's not talking about government welfare here LOL)
27. "It does not matter how slowly you go so long as you do not stop." – Confucius
28. "The heart of man plans his way, but the Lord establishes his steps." Proverbs 16:9
29. "Obstacles are those frightful things you see when you take your eyes off your goal." – Henry Ford

30. "Whatever you do, work heartily, as for the Lord and not for men." Colossians 3:23

Whether it is a scripture verse or a memorable quote, please consider using all of these to stay focused and follow through on what it is that God is leading you to do.

RESCUE STORY 16 – PHIL – THE ATHLETIC COACH AND MISERABLE HUSBAND

Phil came to me feeling hopeless in his marriage. He felt he didn't have anything in common with his wife anymore and everything she did annoyed him. He had story after story about what she had done and how upset it made him.

I asked him about what was good about her and he struggled to come up with anything. He had asked her for years to do things around the house, to keep things tidy, put dishes in the dishwasher "the right way", and pay the bills on time.

She also didn't seem to be interested in romance anymore. She complained it was because he was always nagging her about not doing anything right and she just wasn't attracted to him anymore.

We had a coaching session and I asked him to take the week and go home and write down every thing he could think of that he is grateful for regarding her. He came back the next week feeling totally different. He had pages of things he thought about that she had done and still does that makes him appreciate her more every day.

We aren't used to focusing on the positive in part because we seem to be an entitled society who think other people exist to make us happy instead of the other way around. We don't notice that they wake up, say good morning, give a listening ear, go shopping, go to work, are good to the kids, are loving at times, romantic, unselfish, giving to others, good at fixing stuff and on and on.

He simply shifted his perspective and found the gem he married. Yes, still a diamond in the rough but nevertheless she was his diamond and he found her value that day and never let her forget it.

FOOD FOR THOUGHT

1. Which do you tend to listen to…the Gremlin or the Cheerleader? (My mom would say the angel or the devil).

2. What do you like about the one minute manager? Would you like to be more like this?

3. Think of a time someone did a random act of kindness toward you and how you felt.

4. What random act of kindness could you do? How does it make you feel to think about it?

MORE JOURNALING

CHAPTER 16:

THE 3 G'S AND ADDICTION RECOVERY

Because I am a recovering alcoholic and drug addict myself, I have a deep passion for helping others to recover. I have worked with every single age group, but my focus has become the fastest growing group that is dying from alcohol use disorder...older women.

In fact, I am so concerned about the alcohol and drug problem in our nation that my next book is going to be all about the 3 G's and other recovery tools to help stay clean and sober, so this chapter isn't as long as it might have been!

There are so many challenges for anyone trying to overcome addiction, whether it is alcohol, drugs, food, gambling or anything else. The first step is admitting that you need help and that is not something our society teaches well.

Think back to when your teacher called on you and you didn't know the answer. Or even now, you are in a crowd and someone asks you a question about something in the news and you don't have a clue. How does it feel?

And if you are a person of faith, involved with a community of believers, they will have certain expectations of how you should behave based on their belief system and their sense of "right and wrong" and certainly, not knowing or not doing the 'right thing" is a real problem.

Needless to say it is even more challenging for Christians to admit they have a problem. Same thing with professionals. People think, "you should know." Or they may make fun of you or talk behind your back about you and that hurts.

If you can at least admit you have a problem, you can be Grateful that you have gained some awareness that you have a problem. You can tell yourself you're Good at being open, considering that you might have an issue that you need help with, your Goal would be to take a step and reach out to someone who could help you.

So then you tell yourself, I'm Grateful that there are people who have offered to help me with my drinking problem or my addiction problem. I'm Good at humbling myself so that I can get better. My Goal is to call them today.

You make a phone call, you have a conversation and then you tell yourself I'm Grateful they were there for me. I'm Good at following through with what I say I'm going to do, and my Goal is to stay sober the rest of the day.

So, 20 minutes later you want to "relapse" into whatever that addictive behavior may be, and you say to yourself I'm Grateful I've made it for 20 minutes. I'm Good at staying on track one minute at a time and my Goal is to not drink...use drugs...eat junk food...scroll social media, etc... for the next 20 minutes.

If you are struggling, try to find someone else to call, go to a support group, go for a walk or anything to get your mind off of it. Then, give yourself credit for taking the step

It is all about developing a Self Confidence Loop Builder- SCLB. I just came up with that and wanted to be sure it was my original theory so I did a bit of research and apparently it is!

Don't get my SCLB (pronounced skleb) process theory confused with Brenden Burchard's "competence-confidence loop," which he popularized in 2001.

I had honestly never heard of Burchard's teaching until just this second, but It's the idea that as we learn we gain competence, and as we gain more competence we are more confident to try more, which again grows our competence.

Clearly this is true and fits right in with my model which just goes further into how to build the script needed to reprogram those neural pathways using the 3 G's.

Take note in the rest of these stories how they built their own SCLB's to get out of the muddy rut and create a new pathway by using Gratitude, Good at and Goals self talk to get to where they want to be in life. Read on...

DON'T FORGET TO KEEP WORKING ON YOUR SCLB

Self Confidence Loop Builder

RESCUE STORY #17 – DONNA, THE 55-YEAR OLD ALCOHOLIC AND DRUG ADDICT

I got a call from Donna stating she needed a sober house because she had left her drug addicted boyfriend and needed a safe place. She had been using cocaine and drinking alcohol for a long time and she was done. Her kids weren't speaking to her anymore, she was alienated from her family and she had no support system at all.

Donna struggled for a few months to come to terms with all of her feelings of guilt, shame, hurt, and anger. She relapsed a few times on alcohol but using the things she was learning with the 3 G's, AA and developing a closer relationship with God to make changes, she got better.

She learned that she had a great deal to be grateful for, that she had many gifts and talents to offer the world that she was good at, and that she had goals to get a job and get her dignity, respect and life back.

Donna stayed in our home for almost 2 years. She got a job and did her best but she had developed COPD and had always suffered with depression, anxiety, back issues and other problems so work was nearly impossible for her to maintain full time.

Donna was eventually found to be too disabled to support herself and was awarded disability benefits. She still tried to work part time after she moved into her own apartment. She got a cat, continues to see a counselor and other medical professionals and maintains contact with her family and support system. She has been sober for 10 years.

She was once known as "Donna Downer" because she looked at everything through a negative lens. Once she started using the 3 G's she realized she had a lot to be Grateful for. She realized she had valuable things to offer the world that she was Good at. And at minimum her Goals were to get out of bed in the morning, take care of her cat and send a fun emoji to me which makes my day.

As you can see throughout this book, addiction is a mindset problem at its core. If we could learn to "accept the things we cannot change and change the things we can" like the serenity prayer says, we would be able to be more at peace with living life.

The addiction problem starts when we get it in our minds that we somehow deserve or need a quick fix to our uncomfortable feelings and we learn that alcohol, drugs, sex, spending, gambling, food or God knows what (and He does) will make us feel better... for the moment.

My next book will be on how to use the 3 G's to overcome addiction of any kind. It will be especially geared to you older women who are in the throes of, or have had to deal with the menopausal beast from hell that puts you on an emotional roller coaster and may also drive you to drink or eat incessantly and gripe at everyone you know for no apparent reason while gaining massive quantities of belly fat you can't get rid of and sweating bullets when it 20 below zero!

So... be sure to get on my email list for the release of that book!

PLAY IT TO THE END!
THAT NEXT DRUNK MAY
LAND YOU WHERE YOU
DON'T WANT TO BE

FOOD FOR THOUGHT

1. What areas in your life do you find that you may be a little overindulgent and need to admit what needs to change?

2. What SCLB do you need to develop that will keep you focused on recovery?

3. How can you use the 3 G's in your own words to avoid going down the wrong path

4. What about Donna's story can you relate to?

MORE JOURNALING

CHAPTER 17:

THE 3 G'S IN RELATIONSHIPS AND FAMILIES

Family relationships are challenging and people get desperate to end the pain unless they learn how to deal with it in healthier ways.

In 2023 the U.S. Census determined that 43 million children, a 58% majority, were living with both their birth mother and biological father in a traditional married-couple family. That leaves 42% in chaos because they aren't living with both parents.

What that means is that there are kids who may be going back and forth from parent to parent. One child I worked with had 9 other parental figures in their life moving in and out of their mom or dads homes that they had to deal with. (mom's boyfriends, dad's girlfriends, etc.)

And then there are different apartments in different parts of town, going to different schools, family conflict and a multitude of painful events that they don't know how to deal with.

These traumatic events cause all parties to go through periods of being unwell mentally. We call that "mental illness". Even though people don't want to admit it, the fact remains, whether we are children or adults, we are all ill at times from what is going on in our heads.

Throughout this book I have explained that when we are in pain we seek ways to cope so we can feel better. These coping strategies start long before a break-up, with both the kids and the parents.

Kids notice things. And it is hard for them to cope too, and, unfortunately, they pick up their coping skills from parents who are not always the best examples.

What are some common relationship coping mechanisms? You know. You have undoubtedly been there and done them too. Let's make a list. (PS, this list is why I will always have a job because people need help navigating these things.)

Negative coping in CHILDREN according to research:

1. Withdrawal and isolation (staying in their room, avoiding family and friends)
2. People-pleasing and "parenting" the parent (becoming a little adult/caretaker)
3. Acting out at school or home (anger, defiance, aggression)
4. Somatizing (stomachaches, headaches, sleep problems with no clear medical cause)
5. Numbing with screens (excessive gaming, social media, YouTube, etc.)
6. Self-blame ("It's my fault they're fighting/divorcing/angry")
7. Lying or hiding problems to "keep the peace"
8. Self-harm or risky behaviors (cutting, early sexual activity, dangerous stunts, alcohol/drugs)
9. Emotional shutdown (flat affect, "I don't care," no visible feelings)
10. Overachieving/perfectionism to earn love or avoid conflict

Negative coping in PARENTS:

1. Using alcohol or drugs to escape stress and conflict
2. Staying "busy" constantly (workaholism, over-volunteering) to avoid dealing with pain

3. Yelling, criticizing, or using sarcasm instead of honest, calm communication
4. Stonewalling/silent treatment (shutting down emotionally, refusing to talk)
5. Triangling children (confiding in them about adult problems, making them choose sides)
6. Blaming the child or partner for their own emotions and behavior
7. Passive-aggressive behavior (guilt trips, subtle digs, withholding affection)
8. Avoiding responsibility ("This is just how I am"; refusing to seek help)
9. Over-controlling or over-protective behavior driven by fear and anxiety
10. Emotional cheating or seeking emotional validation outside the family instead of addressing core issues

These behaviors happen in families even if they stay together. The number of healthy parent relationships where their kids say "my parents really love each other and that's the kind of relationship I want" is very rare.

The breakup of parents can have a long-term negative impact on children. A U.S. Census Bureau working paper linked parental divorce to lower income, reduced likelihood of living away from home while attending college, and higher rates of teen pregnancy, incarceration and mortality. Read on for some shocking statistics.

These estimates look at the average effect among children of divorce in early childhood (ages 0-5) which was a bit worse than older children:

- Increased teen births by roughly 60%.
- Increased the likelihood of incarceration by 40%.
- Increased mortality risk at age 25 by 45%.
- Reduced income at age 25 by 9%, and by age 27, by 13%

Clearly these children are "coping" in unhealthy ways because their parents were doing the same.

What does the research show for how parents are coping after a split?

Divorce doesn't just affect the heart emotionally—it can take a toll on the body too like we learned in the chapter on trauma. Studies show that, compared to people who stay married, those who divorce are more likely to struggle with issues like high blood pressure, diabetes, heart problems, and even everyday aches and pains. They also tend to miss more work and find daily tasks harder to manage.

Researchers say this happens mainly for three reasons. First, divorce can strain finances and social support, which makes it harder to afford healthy food, gym memberships, or good medical care.

Second, many people slide into unhealthy coping habits after a breakup—more drinking, smoking, poor eating, and less exercise—exactly the things that wear down the body over time.

Third, ongoing conflict with an ex can keep stress levels high, and chronic stress can disrupt the immune system, heart, and hormones.

My goal as a counselor is to help families to better deal with these conflicts to prevent the pain of separation or divorce on the kids and parents.

Whether you are trying to quit drinking, making a decision about a job or deciding on what you are going to say or do in a relationship with friends, family or coworkers, you have to think of the consequences.

When I finally figured out that if I would just stop for a moment, think, and play the scenario to the end once I picked up that drink, sent that text, said that thing or made that decision, it made a difference in what I did next.

We make decisions based on our momentary feelings. Far too often we don't take the time to consider the pros and cons of how our actions will impact others, including our loved ones. It is human nature to be self protective which is a good thing, but we need to take time to play out the possible end results to the end and then decide if it is really going to be best for us.

So the next time you are going to make a decision, make a pros and cons list and see which side is longer. Play it to the end and sit with it. You will have fewer regrets and many more positive end results.

I have other rescue stories I have already shared about families who have used the 3 G's to turn things around but here is another one.

RESCUE STORY #18 – SUE, THE BATTLE OF AN ALCOHOLIC SPOUSE

John and Sue were on the verge of divorce. John had a drinking problem and just kept moving further and further away from Sue emotionally. Her anger increased as she saw him losing himself in the bottle, quit doing things at home, and had very little to do with her or their child.

As I began working with her on using the 3G's to change her own thinking and look to find the good in him, she responded initially with "I can't find ANYTHING- he does NOTHING at home, he is about to get fired, he doesn't care about me, and is totally selfish. "

I am not sure where we learned it but we seem to have all adopted some of these errors in thinking where we use all or nothing, black and white, exaggerations to describe things. More on the 10 errors in thinking after this story.

I asked her first to write a comprehensive list of everything she was Grateful for Good at, and what her Goals were for herself. She found it hard because John was so negative but she did it.

Then I gave her a harder task and asked her to get more specific and write down what she was Grateful for about her husband, what he was Good at and what Goals did she have to improve their marriage.

At first, she struggled to find things because she was so angry. I asked her to relive their courtship. She realized that he was still in there somewhere, but due to things that were happening in life and losses in his personal, family, and work life, he was coping with alcohol.

She started to focus more on what she did appreciate about him and she told him. She quit complaining and if he did get up and help with any little thing, she let him know how grateful she was and how much it meant to her.

Before long he was doing more and more and feeling better and better about himself. He agreed to come to a session so I could talk with them both and he stated that he did want to quit drinking and he did want to save his marriage.

In just a few months, instead of splitting up, they decided to do something they always dreamed of. They sold their house and decided to travel. They were very excited and grateful that the 3 G's had turned their entire family and life goals around.

She learned through this experience that whatever you appreciate will appreciate (a quote from the book "The Soul of Money: Transforming Your Relationship with Money and Life" by Lynne Twist.

Now, about those 10 errors in thinking I mentioned–

The phrase "10 errors in thinking" usually refers to the list of "cognitive distortions" popularized by psychiatrist Dr. David D. Burns in his book "Feeling Good: The New Mood Therapy". He expanded on the work of Aaron Beck (the father of cognitive therapy).

1. All-or-Nothing Thinking – Seeing things in black-and-white categories. If it's not perfect, it's a total failure.
2. Overgeneralization – Taking one negative event and seeing it as a never-ending pattern ("I always fail," "People always leave me").
3. Mental Filter – Focusing only on the negative details and filtering out the positives.
4. Disqualifying the Positive – Rejecting positive experiences by insisting they "don't count" ("They were just being nice").
5. Jumping to Conclusions – Making negative interpretations without real evidence, including: Mind Reading – Assuming you know what others are thinking. Fortune Telling – Predicting things will turn out badly.
6. Magnification and Minimization – Exaggerating your mistakes or others' successes and downplaying your strengths or achievements.

7. Emotional Reasoning – Assuming that because you feel something, it must be true ("I feel worthless, so I must be worthless").
8. Should Statements – Using "should," "must," or "ought" to pressure yourself or others, often leading to guilt or resentment.
9. Labeling and Mislabeling – Attaching a global, negative label to yourself or others ("I'm a loser," "She's terrible") instead of describing the specific behavior.
10. Personalization and Blame – Taking responsibility for things that aren't fully your fault, or blaming others and refusing to see your part.

As you can see, communication is key to sharing how you are feeling about the relationship and you can demonstrate that in healthy ways… or not. It's up to you.

But I can guarantee you (and I say this gently, with love) that if you take a personal inventory of what comes out of your own mouth you will hear yourself saying ... "You never..." or "You should… "or "Why don't you ever…" or "You always…"

Am I right? Ask your family or friends if you have any of the 10 errors in thinking. Hopefully you will catch yourself more often than you will want to point it out in others.

Now give some thought to what this chapter is about and what you may need to do to make things better in your family and write it down in the food for thought section.

WHATEVER YOU APPRECIATE WILL APPRECIATE

Lynne Twist

FOOD FOR THOUGHT

1. What are some ways that you have coped when you are upset with someone that hasn't been good for you and/or others?

   ____

2. In looking at the 10 errors in thinking, are there any that you may need to work on?

3. Are there things that you have on your gratitude list that you have discovered are gaining in value as you focus more on it? (like toilet paper, LOL)

4. What would legacy would you like to see your family put on your headstone when you die ?

JOURNALING THE 3 G'S AND MORE

CHAPTER 18:

HOW TO CREATE A MENTAL HEALTH FRIENDLY WORKPLACE

DAVE DID IT

We all have to work. Whether we get paid or not is beside the point.

Work can be as little as getting out of bed in the morning and taking care of yourself. And whether you're going to a job or taking care of a family, the reality is that we may not always be motivated to do it.

We have also all been a manager or a boss. It may be a parent, a younger sibling or an employee, but we have influence in how they perform whatever it is we are trying to show them.

People wonder why there is such a turnover in some jobs, and they seem to think it's only because people don't think they get paid enough, but after being a career counselor and working with employers and employees for 15 years with the Department of Workforce Development of Wisconsin, that job satisfaction and retention is about much more than money.

You will probably remember the story earlier in the book about the teachers and the parents that I talked about which are examples of workers and bosses. They found success in using the 3 G's to make changes on the behavior of their children and students.

When I think about transformation in business, and those employers that stand out with the lowest rates of turnover, I think of people like Dave.

Dave retired a few years ago and is now an associate pastor at a church and is making an amazing impact, especially with those parishioners who struggle with addiction and other mental health issues.

Dave did the hiring and the company had really struggled with retaining staff and maintaining a profit because of the constant turnover and people not being reliable.

I picked up the phone when it rang and heard "Linda, it's Dave at XYZ Manufacturing. Can you send me some people who are looking for work that will show up when they are scheduled? "

I said "Dave what kind of skills do these people need?"

"Well," he began, "I'll tell you, if I need them to pound a nail into a board, I will give them a hammer and a banana and ask them which one they should use to be successful, and if they pick the banana, I will give them a second chance and show them how to use the hammer."

It was the best laugh I had all week long, but I knew exactly who to call to find him some reliable people. It was Rhonda at the Marathon County Jail.

Rhonda was my go to person because her job was to help inmates find jobs and transition out of jail successfully. Rhonda was quick to send me several guys who were very happy to get out of jail and earn some money.

Now don't jump to conclusions, or make assumptions (like the 10 errors in thinking we talked about) because I am not saying that people who are in jail don't know a banana from a hammer!

In fact, these guys were all very smart, talented and good hard workers, that is, when they weren't drinking, getting high or breaking the law in some other way.

Unfortunately, the majority of these people still had some bad habits which is what led to their incarceration to begin with but getting a job gave them a chance at a fresh start, and the opportunity to at least indulge in at least getting a pack of cigarettes now and then.

Dave's approach as a manager for the several hundred staff that he was responsible for, included making contact with every single one of them every single day to let them know they were appreciated and that they mattered as people, not just workers.

He would go around and get to know them and ask about their families and things that he could pray about or support them in.

Dave's care and concern made a difference because, for some of these people, he was the only one who cared enough to even ask about how they were doing.

Dave also knew that he would be at risk of having people who were struggling with addiction and may relapse and fail a random drug test or breathalyzer, but he had a plan to address that

Employees who would have otherwise been fired were given the opportunity to join a recovery group that included individual coaching with Dave and a 10-week Bible based recovery program.

This was certainly unprecedented in this company since the owner was not even of the Christian faith, but he let Dave buy Bibles for everyone in the class on the company budget.

Of course, this isn't something that every business can or should do, but Dave developed an evidence based program that showed clearly on the profit and loss report that his approach significantly and positively impacted both attendance and production rates.

Could it be that showing genuine care and concern for people like Jesus said actually makes this much of a difference in a business? This employer told Dave that whatever you're doing, keep doing it because it's working.

So I didn't even know about the 3 G's at this time and neither did Dave, but I want to demonstrate how he actually used it to have the impact that he did on the people that he worked with to get a commitment of loyalty, respect, and their desire to do their best. Check out his influence on this next rescue story.

RESCUE STORY #19 – DION – THE UNEMPLOYED JAILBIRD

As soon as I got the call from Dave, the manager from the factory who was looking for "bodies that will show up to work" I called Rhonda, my job placement representative at the jail, and asked her to send me some people.

The first one to show up was Dion. Unfortunately, he had quite the job history, or lack thereof, because he was a chronic alcoholic who was in and out of jail for drunk driving, disorderly conduct, and other "under the influence" behaviors that don't set well with being a nice obedient community member.

Dion was feeling pretty hopeless and said " I've been a failure my whole life, but I'm willing to try again and see if I can be successful this time." I helped him fill out the application online and I gave Dave a call to let him know that Dion was ready to show up for work.

It didn't take long before Dion was skipping his way out of the jail and jumping on his bike to ride the several miles to work. (Well… he probably wasn't skipping. He was probably walking like a cool dude who was just chillin' without a care in the world despite the jail door slamming behind him. LOL) He was Grateful for the opportunity and really felt hopeful.

Since he had struggled with his sobriety for so long, he took advantage of the classes that Dave had going and very much appreciated the encouragement that he got at work.

Dion had never been more supported, at least not that he could remember, nor had he ever been sober long enough to appreciate anything, but this was different.

Dion had been to treatment several times, but to be honest, being in treatment is totally different from being out in the world where you're still faced with temptation. Now, he also had money so he could have stopped to get some booze along the way, but he realized that he really had a chance to make a change.

Between the security of being in jail at night and not having the freedom to drink, and getting the constant encouragement and support at work from Dave and others who came to appreciate him as a team member, he realized that sobriety was really worth it.

It was through Dave's example and support, and helping him to realize what to be Grateful for, what he was Good at, and how to reach his Goals that Dion completed his time in jail and continued to work for this company for as long as I knew him.

I wonder if you have ever thought about being that kind of example or choosing to turn your life around in such a way? Maybe it's some food for thought.

FOOD FOR THOUGHT

1. What kinds of experiences have you had at work or school that have impacted you in negative ways because of what people said or did to you or others.

   ____
   ____
   ____

2. What are some positive memories you have about work or school and what did people say or do that made you feel good.

   ____
   ____
   ____

3. How could you show people that you care in more consistent and positive ways?

   ____
   ____
   ____

4. Who will you begin reaching out to today to put the 3 G's into action?

   ____
   ____
   ____

JOURNALING THE 3 G'S AND MORE

CHAPTER 19:

3 G'S SPIRITUALITY, FAITH AND RELIGION

All religions share some common similarities. They are centered around beliefs about life, meaning, purpose, and often a higher power or spiritual truth.

While religions may differ in their teachings, traditions, and practices, they often help people understand the world, guide their choices, and give them a sense of hope, identity, and belonging.

In one way or another, everyone has beliefs. Those beliefs may be religious, spiritual, moral, or personal. People are naturally drawn to others who share similar values and beliefs, and they often come together in groups or communities to worship, learn, pray, celebrate, support one another, and grow in their understanding.

These gatherings may happen in churches, temples, mosques, synagogues, homes, or other community spaces, but the common thread is connection. People find comfort and strength in being with others who believe as they do.

Unfortunately, some people have a hard time accepting those who don't believe exactly as they do and this happens even within the church. This is why the Christian religion, for example, has an estimated 45,000 different denominations!

It all came about because somebody didn't agree with somebody else so they just stomped off and started their own church with their own set of rules and regulations that they felt more accurately interpreted scripture. Everyone wants to be "right" yet they are missing the big picture.

Jesus came to bring peace to the world, not conflict. If you look at the teachings of all the other religions out there, love and kindness is foundational to all of them.

Jesus tried very hard to get the disciples to bring unity but we are a prideful people and it is hard to consider that maybe it is better to love than to hate someone else for being different.

In fact, almost every other religion adheres to the basic tenet of the 3 G's, including showing gratitude, believing that we all have talent, abilities, experiences, interest, and value that can benefit the world.

They also all believe that we should be seeking to grow and become better people. We should help one another through setting an intention (goal) to help others in the best ways we can.

In my counseling and coaching, I have worked with many people that have been traumatized by their experiences in organized religion and it is hard to know how to help them.

They are confused about God, faith and religion because leaders in their religious faith have shamed them, taken advantage of them, stripped them of their dignity, used and abused them in a variety of ways.

They have not demonstrated the love of God that draws people to be their best and use their gifts and talents to share their faith with others.

I grew up in a Lutheran Church and have been a part of a wide variety of other churches over the years, including American Baptist, Southern Baptist, non-denominational and various charismatic churches and I am not partial to any of the 45,000+ denominations out there but I do have some fond memories of pastors that have been an example to me that I have tried to follow after.

THE CHURCH HAS LEFT THE BUILDING

Pastor Dale, Pastor Aaron and Evangelist Saul–

I met Pastor Dale over 40 years ago when I was in a very wounded and depressed state of mind. I had gone through a painful divorce and was now a single mom struggling financially, and not knowing where to turn.

I was no longer in a church since the pastor of the church where I had been going for many years with my husband made a sexual pass when I went to him for counseling and support.

Of course I was cautious and felt extremely rejected by many of my Christian church friends who were no longer reaching out to me since I wasn't going to their church anymore. They knew nothing of what had happened to me and they didn't seem to care.

I decided to visit this little country school where Pastor Dale's church met. I felt very welcomed in this casual environment where everyone seemed to feel like they were part of a family.

People were given the opportunity to share their prayer requests and their wins for the week where they could have a moment of feeling good about life, even when it was tough. There was singing, study and prayer and church members were invited to be involved whenever and wherever possible.

As Pastor Dale learned that I played guitar and sang and went to Bible College he quickly got me involved in using the gifts God has given me. It gave me purpose in my pain.

At the end of each Sunday service we were all invited to stay for the weekly "pot-luck." Some of you are wondering what that is, aren't you?

I DIGRESS- AGAIN! What is a potluck? A term originating in the 16th century that an unexpected guest must come to understand that if they dropped in on someone they were at the mercy of whatever was in the host's pot to eat... pot-luck. In the last couple of centuries the term has evolved into more of a communal covered dish that everyone brings to a meal to share with others and again... with the hope that everyone isn't bringing the same dish.

Back to Pastor Dale. In this little church there were very few of us that had much money so it was indeed luck if there was anything at all in the pot, if we even had a pot to bring (or to pee in like us mid-westerner back woods folks say. LOL.:... Don't get me started on where that saying comes from.

Many never brought anything to share but they had their several children in tow coming to eat, more than likely, their only real meal of the day. But that was OK. Often, the majority of the food was macaroni and cheese and ramen noodles but we were together and we were not being judged.

Many of us came from substance abuse backgrounds, divorce and criminal records. I had avoided the criminal record part because I never got caught driving drunk or being disorderly. (WHEW!)

One of the couples that were there had come out of a satanic cult where they had done blood sacrifices and much more, but we all found a new start at this church.

Unfortunately Dale moved out of state and the little church was gone. He left a mark in Wausau, Wisconsin and we will never be the same. And that's a good thing! (Not that he had moved but that we were changed... but you knew what I meant, right?)

PASTOR AARON WINOWISKI

It took me many years to find another pastor that "felt like home." Fortunately, I did and his name is Aaron Winowiski and he is the Pastor of New Day Christian Church in Weston, Wisconsin.

My step-daughter Crystal told Ralph and I about New Day because it was meeting at the school where our granddaughter was attending. The worship team started the service and they did all the songs I used to play at other churches where I had been the worship leader.

Then Pastor Aaron came on stage in his tennis shoes and jeans and had a sense of humor and a down to earth approach that really made us feel like we were going to be a good fit. It was a few months later that I was asked to be on the worship team and play guitar and sing which I really enjoyed.

What I love about his church is the idea that "the church" isn't a building. It is the people and the slogan "the church has left the building" comes from a service that our church provides every summer where we nominate friends, neighbors or others that we know that need help with things like yardwork, painting, repair, etc and then people from the church volunteer to go do the work.

The goal is to "show the love of Christ" and then through those relationships, share the good news of the gospel. Showing love comes first, not bashing them over the head with judgmentalism using scripture as a shame tool.

EVANGELIST SAUL GILL

When Covid-19 hit the United States and we were no longer meeting face to face, some of us found the online platform to be a great opportunity to invite people "to church" from all over the world.

Besides Pastor Bonigala Sam Daniel from India, who I already talked about in an earlier chapter who is another example that could be in this chapter, I met Evangelist Saul Gill from Pakistan.

Brother Gill joins us frequently for our church service online at New Day even though he is 76,000 miles away. He brings other people to watch with him in their humble places along with the orphans he cares for.

Brother Gill is the most active member of our 3 G's group on our Facebook speaktomegodimlistening page and he is by far my biggest most consistent support in everything I do online.

Brother Gill shows his love and encouragement through posting and messaging every single day for the last 4+ years and he has never missed a day except when the floods in Pakistan caused them to flee and they had no power or internet connection or when he is in the hospital or at work with no cell reception.

As Christians, we are called to "go even to the ends of the earth" to share the love of God and my "mission work" for my church is largely online while my church family here in my community is going out on prayer walks sharing Christ with strangers. We all have our part to do and we don't judge each other because it's different.

That's another attribute that Pastor Aaron, along with these other men have demonstrated. Not being judgmental toward others. With the massive division in the church over politics, and losing many of our church members over the Covid-19 crises and the church board's decision to follow the "shelter in place" guidelines, he has been able to share God's word without talking negatively about anyone or "taking sides." That is a hard line to walk comfortably.

If we are going to reach others we also have to be relateable. To do that we have to be willing to be humble and transparent. For a pastor to admit from the pulpit (or wherever they are speaking from) that he has ADHD and doesn't always pick up on social cues and isn't comfortable calling people out of the blue, truly shows humility and it is a rare quality in a pastor and I really appreciate it.

Through Pastor Aaron's openness in sharing that he has weaknesses and he relies on the rest of the body of Christ to use their gifts and talents to fill the gaps, we can collaboratively further the kingdom and show the world that there can be unity and love.

My point is- that the church, at least the Christian church, should be the example of the sacrificial, putting others first example of the Savior we claim to follow. If we use the 3 G's to focus on being Grateful for one another, encourage people by using the gifts they are Good at and supporting them in reaching their Goals, the church will fill the gaps that our government can't and none of us individually ever will.

RESCUE STORY #20 – TJ – THE VETERAN WITH NO HOME AND NO HOPE

I first met TJ about 17 years ago when he was referred to our program for assistance dealing with his mental health and transitioning from homelessness and unemployment to self sufficiency.

TJ came with baggage, Not the suitcase kind. The childhood kind that led him to join the military and try to make the best of it but it was a challenge and he was discharged because of his mental health they determined was not service related so he got no benefits.

The family was less than supportive so he had no one but us, so we became like his parents in many ways. He was in his early 20's when he moved out of our transition home and got involved with a woman and had his first child. Things didn't work out and they separated.

It wasn't long before he got involved with another woman and they had two children together. Between having Bi-Polar disorder, PTSD, Anxiety and a slew of other alphabet diagnosis, he struggled with substance abuse on and off for years. The toxic relationships he continued to find himself in, or help create eventually left him single, broke, without his children and homeless.

A rollercoaster of other experiences, including a 10 year relationship that ended badly, a battle with drugs and a realization that PTSD needed to be addressed led to an amazing change.

He went back to school and got his first degree in Civil Engineering and now he is back at our home doing amazing and getting another degree in Software Development where his GPA is about 3.7. He is also working and being responsible for himself, his cat and everything he needs in life.

TJ is no longer a self-centered demanding and difficult young man, he is a kind, appreciative, intelligent and supportive housemate that has brought joy to our other resident and to us as we see that being like "Jesus with skin on" like one of my friends described our role as Christians, has made a difference.

TJ now talks about wanting to be more like Jesus and following God's plan for his life rather than just being selfish. He is financially responsible and conscientious and learning the 3 G's back in 2008 has helped him to get to where he is today.

Like they say in AA- It works if you work it…it doesn't if you don't. Change can and does happen if you learn from your mistakes, let go of what you can't control, and forge a new neural pathway with a clear and God focused direction.

IF WE WERE TO TREAT OTHERS THE WAY WE WOULD LIKE THEM TO TREAT US, THE WORLD WOULD BE A MUCH BETTER, MORE PEACEFUL AND SAFE PLACE TO BE

Follow the Golden Rule from

Luke 6:31

FOOD FOR THOUGHT

1. Do you have any "church hurt" that has left you not trusting in God or wanting to be a part of a religious fellowship or be cautious about getting involved?

2. How have you seen people of faith use their beliefs to help others? How did you feel?

3. How has your spiritual beliefs impacted you to be a positive impact in the world?

4. What are you going to start doing different to be a positive influence and support to those around you?

JOURNALING THE 3 G'S AND MORE

CHAPTER 20:

MAKING THE SPIRITUAL CONNECTION TO LEAVE YOUR LEGACY?

DEFINING A SPIRITUAL CONNECTION

What is a "spiritual connection?" I always ask my clients if they have any "spiritual beliefs or practices" and most of them will say "no I don't go to church."

I was curious what I would get as a definition so I asked Hope (this is the name I gave my ChatGPT responder because I have lots of questions about stuff and she's smarter than me) and this is what I got for the definition of "spiritual."

Spiritual refers to something related to the spirit, soul, or inner essence of a person—often involving:

- A connection to something greater than oneself (God, the divine, the sacred, the universe)
- Inner experiences like peace, meaning, purpose, and transcendence
- A personal relationship with faith or the sacred
- Values, beliefs, and practices that give life meaning and direction

- The non-material aspects of human experience (as opposed to the physical or material)

So what then is “religion?” Again...the search brought me this difference.

Religion generally refers to an organized system of beliefs and practices that help people relate to the divine or the sacred. It often includes things like:

1. Doctrines/teachings (what is believed)
2. Rituals/practices (how people worship or live their faith)
3. Community (shared identity, belonging, and support)
4. Traditions (passed-down customs and ways of doing things)

In contrast to spirituality (which is often more personal and individually explored), religion tends to be more structured and communal—though many people experience both in a personal way.

As I stated in earlier chapters, the 12 steps of AA got its start with a Christian missionary but what then do you do with people from other religions or who don’t have a belief in the God of the Bible? And even if they do believe in the God of the Bible, their interpretation of how to make a God connection and hear God speak can be very different.

You see there is a BIG difference between religion and relationship. You can adopt a belief system that includes a bunch of rules or principles, but that does not constitute a relationship with a living being.

Religion is like having a photograph but a relationship is like talking to the person in the picture. Or it’s having a map to follow which is nothing like having a guide who can direct you because they have been there.

Some people think that just because they quote scripture or say “I am a born again Christian” or they carry a Bible, go to their house of worship every week, say they are prophets, or wear religious jewelry or clothes that the rest of the world is going to think that they are actually true representatives of Christianity that gives them the right, or even obligation to tell everyone else how to live their lives.

Sorry if that hurts, but let's take a look at what Jesus himself said in the last few chapters of Matthew about the religious leaders and WOW... he didn't mince words either!

Buckle up...this is a long one and may cause some angst amongst the religious leaders and their followers of our day...I am sure you can easily see how what is happening in America these days relates.

Matthew Chapter 23:1-6 is titled in the ESV "Seven Woes to the Scribes and Pharisees

Then Jesus said to the crowds and to his disciples,

"The scribes and the Pharisees sit on Moses' seat, so do and observe whatever they tell you, but not the works they do. For they preach, but do not practice. They tie up heavy burdens, hard to bear, and lay them on people's shoulders, but they themselves are not willing to move them with their fingers.

They do all their deeds to be seen by others. For they make their phylacteries broad and their fringes long, and they love the place of honor at feasts and the best seats in the synagogues..."

He gives a bunch of examples in verses 7-22 then Jesus says;

Matthew 23:23 "Woe to you, scribes and Pharisees, hypocrites! For you tithe mint and dill and cumin, and have neglected the weightier matters of the law: justice and mercy and faithfulness. These you ought to have done, without neglecting the others."

Then in Matthew 25 he gets real about us not being "religious on the outside" but actually doing what He has asked regarding justice, mercy and faith. This is the chapter that our entire ministry to the homeless veterans, ex-convicts, addicts and alcoholics was based on and what I do in my coaching business today.

The chapter gives many examples of comparison between religious leaders and true followers. He talks about those who are going to be honored in heaven and those who are not and boy this will be quite the shock to people around the world but I hope my fellow American

Christians are looking at these verses and praying about what it is really saying.

THE SHEEP AND THE GOATS

31 "When the Son of Man comes in his glory, and all the angels with him, then he will sit on his glorious throne. 32 Before him will be gathered all the nations, and he will separate people one from another as a shepherd separates the sheep from the goats. 33 And he will place the sheep on his right, but the goats on the left. 34 Then the King will say to those on his right, 'Come, you who are blessed by my Father, inherit the kingdom prepared for you from the foundation of the world. 35 For I was hungry and you gave me food, I was thirsty and you gave me drink, I was a stranger and you welcomed me, 36 I was naked and you clothed me, I was sick and you visited me, I was in prison and you came to me.' 37 Then the righteous will answer him, saying, 'Lord, when did we see you hungry and feed you, or thirsty and give you drink? 38 And when did we see you a stranger and welcome you, or naked and clothe you? 39 And when did we see you sick or in prison and visit you?' 40 And the King will answer them, 'Truly, I say to you, as you did it to one of the least of these my brothers,[f] you did it to me.'

41 "Then he will say to those on his left, 'Depart from me, you cursed, into the eternal fire prepared for the devil and his angels. 42 For I was hungry and you gave me no food, I was thirsty and you gave me no drink, 43 I was a stranger and you did not welcome me, naked and you did not clothe me, sick and in prison and you did not visit me.' 44 Then they also will answer, saying, 'Lord, when did we see you hungry or thirsty or a stranger or naked or sick or in prison, and did not minister to you?' 45 Then he will answer them, saying, 'Truly, I say to you, as you did not do it to one of the least of these, you did not do it to me.' 46 And these will go away into eternal punishment, but the righteous into eternal life."

OUCH!! Is Jesus that mean? No, He is that loving to ALL mankind, not just certain people. His point is that there are consequences to not following His example because that is what a Christian is... a Christ follower. Like the scripture said, He is the ONLY King, and His direction can bring peace and unity to the world, if we would only listen.

Think about it... If we all helped each other to meet each other's basic needs like food, clothing, water, housing, health care like Jesus commands us, we wouldn't be in a government shutdown today arguing over whether or not we should help those in need or give help to those that were not born in America. ... Just sayin'...

SO HOW DO WE KNOW WHAT GOD'S WILL IS AND WHEN TO HELP OTHERS

Obviously we can't help everyone. Jesus said there would always be poor people, but the good news is that God has a plan for all of us to do what He knows others need.

And yes, there is logic about giving to others and not enabling them. If you remember the rescue story about Niron he talked about having us "give him a hand up, not a hand-out" which means that we may need help to get to where God wants us, but we have to do our part.

I have a tendency to do too much for people which sometimes hinders them from being responsible for themselves, and that is not good. The bible warns us "Do not give dogs what is holy, and do not throw your pearls before pigs, lest they trample them underfoot and turn to attack you".

It has taken me a very long time, especially in my business, to understand the saying that "people don't show up if they have no skin in the game."

To get anywhere in life there needs to be sacrifice. If people aren't ready and willing to do their part, I have other people waiting in line who want what I have to offer. I have to let people go until they are ready to do what it takes, including money and time.

God has given all of us the skill, training, talent, love and compassion that we have to share with others. If they don't value what we have to offer and use it to better themselves then we are wasting the "pearls" that God has given us.

The best way we can help ourselves and others is to make that simple spiritual connection. I truly believe God is big enough to convince anyone He chooses which way to go in life. I will do my part to lead when I can but the rest is up to each individual.

HEARING GOD SPEAK

I have a pretty simple formula that I came up with to make that connection to begin a journey. Whether you aren't sure there even is a God and you are pretty sure you hate organized religion that is fine. Start here.

This is what I did to write my meditation book "Speak to Me God" I'm Listening-365 Daily Meditations for Those Who Want to Hear God Answer Life's Toughest Questions. It will work for you too.

1) Believe in God

Do you believe there is a higher power that communicates with us and has given us guidelines in which to live? What are those guidelines? For me, it is the Bible and whatever message I get must be consistent with what the Bible has already said. God is not going to tell us to lie, cheat and steal. If you are seeking direction the assumption is that you believe you don't have the answers and God does. Our confusion comes when we have no belief that there is a God who can and will communicate with us. If you don't believe in the Bible but have some other faith what is it and do you believe your higher power can speak to you?

2) Be Open and prepared

Eliminate distractions and put on some meditation music, light an aromatic candle or do whatever helps you get focused. Get a pen and paper or your electronic gadget you can write with- I use my computer and save it on Google Drive so I can access it at any time to reread it or add to it. I also use my phone if I don't have my computer and I dictate into my phone instead of typing the tiny keyboard. Studies do show, however, that paper pencil stuff stimulates your brain in different ways giving opportunity for deeper thought and reflection.

3) Know what you need

Every day we get up with things on our minds that we need answers to. Which one is the most relevant? That's what you may want to focus on. God cares about everything that bothers us and He has a solution but if we never slow down long enough to realize what the problem is and give it to God, nothing will change.

4) Find a relevant scripture verse that relates to your challenge

Once you identify what the main issue is, try doing a google search on the challenge you are seeking direction on. Add "Bible" to the search and you will get many verses to choose from. Pick the one that resonates with you the most. It is always good to check the context though. You don't want to just randomly pick a verse like "go build an ark" and think it's a message you need to do today.

5) Pray

Just talk to God and tell Him your problem and ask Him to speak to you. Keep in mind you are focusing on YOUR problem and you are not asking God to change others...you are asking Him to change YOU and give YOU direction and support.

6) Wait and Listen

With a pen in hand or an electronic gadget at your fingertips just begin typing or speaking the words that enter your mind. Don't judge them, don't try to say the right thing. It's not about you. This is God trying to speak to you directly and you can't judge that. This is the holy spirit working in and through you. You will know when He has finished His message to you. Go back and read it and it will probably feel like someone else wrote this because in essence, someone else did!. I promise you though, if you do this daily you will find that your relationship is growing deeper, your anxiety will go down because your faith has increased by knowing that God can handle whatever you are concerned about.

7) Respond to God

When you ask God to answer your prayers you need to respond to Him when He answers. At minimum give Him thanks for speaking to you in that way. You also need to make a decision if you are going to do what His instruction is telling you to do. If He says "fear not" are you going to believe Him and let go of your fear? This process is a two-way street...you ask, God answers, you respond.

SPEAK TO ME GOD, I'M LISTENING

When I put my daily meditations into my book "Speak to Me God I'm Listening-365 Daily Meditations for Those Who Want to Hear God Answer Life's Toughest Questions" I broke it into 5 different sections.

I find the 12 step program to give me a great structure for personal growth and transformation no matter what challenge I am dealing with so I include a step each day.

Next I share the struggle I am having, then I find a relevant scripture, I say a prayer and then I ask God to speak to me about the topic and I write it down. Finally, I make a decision if I am going to respond to what He says.

Here is the very first one He gave me to put in on January 1st. I guess if you got this far in this book it is because you are wanting to make a change so this one is quite fitting for a new year's resolution.

JANUARY 1

RESOLUTION AGAIN?

STEP 1- We admitted we were powerless over our dependencies and that our lives had become unmanageable.

CHALLENGE

Today is the first day of the rest of your life, and like most of us, we make resolutions to change, which according to one definition, means "the action of solving a problem, dispute, or contentious matter." Studies show that 45% of people make resolutions, but only 8% keep them and most of those who fail, do so after only one week! The first step is the honest admission that we are powerless and that our lives have become unmanageable, but we can't stop there, or we will get discouraged and fail. We must also know and accept that there is a God (someone bigger and smarter than we are) who loves us and can free us from our insanity and shame and give us victory over the temptations that we face every day that could sabotage our success! Are we willing to consider that there is someone who can help us more than we have been able to help ourselves?

HOPE

"So humble yourselves under the mighty power of God, and at the right time, He will lift you up in honor." (1 Peter 5:6)

PRAYER

God, show me how to swallow my pride and admit that I need You. I want to do Your will, but I don't know how to accept Your help. Please show me.

SPEAK TO ME GOD`

My Child,

It was My Spirit that moved you to realize that you needed to make a change, and it is My Spirit that will help you to overcome the temptations that you will face. Nothing is beyond My abilities, but you must humble yourself and accept the experience, strength, and hope of those that I have sent that have gone before you and have overcome their challenges. All things are possible if you only believe!

RESPONSE

God, today, I will rely on Your Holy Spirit to help me believe in Your ability to overcome all my troubles.

WHERE WILL YOU GO FROM HERE?

So we are at the end of this book but I hope you aren't at the end of making the change you know you needed to make when you picked up this book. You picked it up because God led you here and now He is asking you to do something about what you have learned.

Will you? Will you do the 3 G's every day and reflect on your day every night before you go to bed looking at all the great blessings of the day?

Will you focus on the positives instead of sitting in the muddy rut of rotten potatoes?

Will you take time to figure out your purpose and begin living it to your best ability?

Will you reach out to those God has put in front of you to give you HOPE (Help Opportunity Praise Encouragement?)

I can already hear some of you saying "I have been trying to do that for years and I am a failure."

Or perhaps you are saying "this is way too hard and unrealistic to even start."

So in a nutshell, we need to accept the grace God offers us. We are each on our own spiritual journey and I truly believe that if we ask Him which way to go He will tell us. No judgment of each other needed.

Doing it alone has been proven scientifically to not be as effective. We need each other, remember what I said in that chapter? So reach out. Let me, or someone else help you find your way to who God created you to be and do.

In closing, today is the first day of the rest of your life. Use it and you will be blessed in return. Let me share one more rescue story with you before we wrap up.

RESCUE STORY #21 – MARGIE – THE STRUGGLING OLDER SINGLE MOM

I met Margie almost 40 years ago when a mutual friend called me from jail and asked me to come and bail her and Margie out because they had been picked up for a drunk driving accident.

Our friend Samantha already had legal stuff going so she had to stay in jail, but since this was Margie's first time in the police department, she was free to go if someone would come and pick her up so I did.

I didn't know her from a hole in the ground (hmmm that's a weird saying…oops..random thought) but I let her stay at my house under one condition, she had to get up and go to church with me the next day.

She was black and blue from the car accident that they had had during their drunken episode the night before and she was massively hung over, but she dragged herself with me anyway.

Margie made a God connection and began changing her life and following God. I did not have a lot of contact with her until about 20 years ago when we connected back up again. She came to the job center and was looking for help getting into childcare. It's what she had always wanted.

I helped her out as much as I could in my role as the job center counselor and then again, lost touch until she got pregnant with her daughter and she reached out again.

It was quite the shock to have gotten pregnant in her mid 40s and she was not prepared financially, mentally, or physically to raise a child alone, but she really didn't have a choice.

She also realized how hard it was to be a single parent so she started an organization called Parents Helping Parents - Where Hands Meet Hearts on Facebook 13 years ago and today she has over 3000 members that help each other to find things that they can't afford to get for themselves.

Whether it's baby formula or money for gas to get to work or medicine for a sick child, this organization of parents helping parents is absolutely astounding. I was so impressed with her work that I nominated her for the Jefferson award, which is our community's way of honoring people who have given an important contribution.

Margie has a lot of health issues and she has struggled with her weight for years. She quit smoking quit drinking quit doing drugs but for many of us, food becomes our go to stress reliever. We don't need alcohol or drugs in the house but we do have to eat and it is hard to stay focused, especially for us ADHDer's like Margie and I, but that didn't hinder her from moving forward and being a help to others.

It takes guts to be overweight and get on Facebook or Instagram or TikTok and work out, but her videos have touched thousands and thousands of people as she shares her journey. She has never given up trying even though now she can't walk much at all, but she presses on with her faith and hope in God.

Margie was also one of my biggest supporters when my last book came out and would call me at times crying about how she felt I had written it for her or had specifically chosen a particular reading to email her when it wasn't me at all. It was God.

I know this is a longer story but it's worth telling. Margie hasn't gotten to where she wants to be in life, but she is doing her very best to use the 3 G's and the Word of God to do her best to be a Faucet of Hope to the rest of us and a great mom to her daughter. I know she is praying that for you as well because that is just who she is and what she does.

IN CLOSING

So with that being said, I want you all to know that my prayers are with you and if you need more help and I'm dead and gone, you can find a ton of videos of Linda's life recovery lessons on YouTube or another random places

God bless you, and please do a review on Amazon or wherever you can and pass this on. Thanks!

Linda

FOOD FOR THOUGHT

1. What are the main things you have learned from this book that you will use?

____

____

____

2. How can you use this information to help those around you.?

____

____

____

3. Who could you ask to help you in making some of these mind, body, spirit change?

____

____

____

4. What are you going to do to get started?

____

____

____

JOURNALING THE 3 G'S AND MORE

____

____

____

____

____

____

____

____

____

DOING THE 3 G'S EVERY DAY WITH NO EXCUSES!

I have heard the excuse of "But I can't think of anything, so I decided to offer a "butectomy" and take the 'but" out of your way. Here are 365 of each of the 3 G's. One of my clients asked me to do a pull jar so she could just pull one out if she couldn't think of anything. Another client asked me to do cards of the What Would Linda Say one liners. Let me know if you are interested and keep an eye out! Maybe I will do a talking Bobblehead! LOL!

GRATITUDE LIST:

1. Family (moms, dad, siblings, grandparents etc)
2. Friends
3. Health
4. A home to live in
5. Clean water
6. Hygiene products like toilet paper
7. Freedom
8. Education
9. Love
10. Nature
11. Sunshine
12. Laughter
13. Music
14. Art
15. Books including the Bible)
16. Electricity
17. Internet
18. Food
19. Warm clothes
20. A good night's sleep
21. A comfortable bed
22. Coffee/Tea
23. A car or transportation
24. Memories
25. Babies
26. Safety
27. Opportunities
28. Kindness of strangers
29. Technology

30. Pets
31. Being alive
32. Deodorant (smelling good)
33. Shoes
34. Transportation
35. Creativity
36. Imagination
37. Strength
38. Motivation
39. The seasons
40. Rainbows
41. Technology
42. Healthcare
43. Humor
44. Sunsets
45. Sunrises
46. Quiet moments
47. Warm blankets
48. Hugs
49. Compliments
50. Community
51. Road trips
52. Learning new skills
53. Achievements
54. Teamwork
55. Gardens
56. Fresh fruits
57. Grandma's recipes
58. Cozy pyjamas
59. Holidays

60. Starry nights
61. Conversations
62. Empathy
63. Traditions
64. Celebrations
65. Clean clothes
66. Optimism
67. Forgiveness
68. Personal growth
69. Faith
70. Inner peace
71. Support systems
72. Mentors
73. Fresh starts
74. Sunny days
75. Cloudy days
76. Snow (if you like it)
77. Adventures
78. Peace of mind
79. Fireplaces
80. Candles
81. Sweet treats
82. Fresh flowers
83. Cozy socks
84. Parks
85. Mountains
86. Forests
87. Rivers
88. Beaches
89. Libraries

90. Museums
91. Theater
92. Photography
93. Journals
94. Moments of courage
95. Kind gestures
96. Smiles
97. The internet
98. Safe travels
99. The ocean
100. Fresh starts
101. Your senses (sight, smell, touch, taste, hearing)
102. Farmers
103. Nurses and doctors
104. Entrepreneurs
105. Teachers
106. Volunteers
107. Soldiers
108. Public servants
109. Scientists
110. Clean energy
111. New experiences
112. Cozy sweaters
113. Hot soup
114. Picnic baskets
115. Board games
116. The sound of rain
117. Retreats
118. Clean sheets
119. Surprise gifts

120. New friends
121. Old friends
122. Learning from mistakes
123. Acts of service
124. Generosity
125. Clarity
126. Communication
127. Dreams
128. Lazy Sundays
129. Bookstores
130. Farmers markets
131. Festivals
132. Cultural experiences
133. Heritage
134. Technology
135. Clothes
136. Nutritious meals
137. Hot showers
138. Sunshine
139. Love notes
140. Positive feedback
141. Memories
142. Clear skies
143. Air conditioning
144. Heating
145. Roof over head
146. A sense of belonging
147. Neighborhood
148. Cleanliness
149. Togetherness

150. Personal space
151. Science
152. Mathematics
153. History
154. Freedom of expression
155. Gardens
156. Trees
157. Flowers
158. Animals
159. Family gatherings
160. Adventure trips
161. Mountains
162. Beaches
163. Traveling
164. Photography
165. Art
166. Personal development
167. Life coaches
168. Self-awareness
169. Mindfulness
170. Meditation
171. Yoga
172. Heart-to-heart talks
173. Old photographs
174. Poetry
175. Christmas lights
176. Birthday cakes
177. Wedding rings
178. Bike rides
179. Sports

180. Inspirational quotes
181. Determination
182. Innovation
183. Free will
184. Diversity
185. Cooking
186. Baking
187. Smell of fresh bread
188. The sound of waves
189. Feeling understood
190. Children's laughter
191. Simple pleasures
192. Listening to stories
193. Fireworks
194. Charity
195. Love
196. Empathy
197. Adventure
198. Courage
199. Personal growth
200. Community
201. The moon
202. The smell of fresh rain
203. The taste of chocolate
204. Fresh vegetables
205. Furniture
206. Pets
207. A moment of silence
208. Personal space
209. Home-cooked meals

210. Gratitude journals
211. Shared experiences
212. Unexpected kindness
213. Crisp fall air
214. Winter's first snow
215. Summer breezes
216. Spring blossoms
217. Histories and stories
218. Freedom to choose
219. Forgiveness
220. Second chances
221. Wishes
222. Night skies
223. Garden fresh herbs
224. Freshly baked cookies
225. Holidays
226. Birthdays
227. Leaps of faith
228. Patience
229. Curious children
230. Aspirations
231. Motivation
232. Acceptance
233. Rediscovered joys
234. Sharing
235. Receiving
236. New beginnings
237. Breath of fresh air
238. Dreams turned reality
239. Tiny miracles

240. Hot chocolate
241. Snowflakes
242. Kaleidoscope
243. Daydreams
244. Clean environments
245. Eco-awareness
246. New shoes
247. Hats and scarves
248. Scarves
249. Reasons to smile
250. Growth opportunities
251. Music that moves
252. Creative moments
253. Trust
254. Healing
255. Fresh perspectives
256. Transitions
257. Lucky breaks
258. Sharing meals
259. Journaling
260. Candlelight
261. Bedtime stories
262. Rediscovery
263. Nostalgic moments
264. Family history
265. Art supplies
266. That perfect hug
267. Summer picnics
268. Dresses and ties
269. A child's curiosity

270. Remembering names
271. A child's first words
272. Snow angels
273. Sandcastles
274. Walking under the stars
275. Successful efforts
276. Acts of bravery
277. Unconditional love
278. Swimming pools
279. Cozy cafes
280. Waterfalls
281. Peaking mountains
282. Resting my eyes
283. Hot tea on a cold day
284. Peaceful protests
285. Morning runs
286. Afternoon naps
287. Educational podcasts
288. Documentaries
289. Global cultures
290. Personal philosophies
291. Stories of survival
292. Simple recipes
293. Fireflies
294. Shooting stars
295. Helping hands
296. Tales of adventure
297. Folk tales
298. A hand to hold
299. Serendipity

300. Positive self-talk
301. Aromatherapy
302. Aromas
303. Sustainable solutions
304. Well-being
305. Confidence boosts
306. Twin rainbows
307. Long drives
308. Favorite songs
309. Life's fairy tales
310. Lazy afternoons
311. Grain of hope
312. Fountains
313. Good habits
314. Sustainable living
315. Renewable energy
316. Electric cars
317. Artistic expression
318. Lasting impressions
319. Blossoming friendships
320. The gentle breeze
321. Local foods
322. Anticipation of possibilities
323. Nectarines
324. Pelicans
325. New languages
326. Warm welcomes
327. Breezy summer days
328. Wind chimes
329. Acapella groups

330. A bugle call
331. Sightseeing
332. Navigation systems
333. 12 Step Programs
334. Eco-conscious communities
335. Countless subjects to learn
336. Game days
337. HOPE (Help Opportunity Praise Encouragement)
338. Kites and airballoons
339. New Year's resolutions
340. Radiating smiles
341. 2nd hand stores
342. Celebrating with loved ones
343. Sipping smoothies
344. Whistling tunes
345. A day of rest and relaxation
346. Cameras
347. Making memories
348. A fresh pair of socks
349. Home-made crafts
350. Cardboard castles
351. Puzzles
352. Fellowship with others
353. Hometown pride
354. Care providers
355. The scent of pine
356. Comedians to make you laugh
357. Inspirational speakers
358. Charities
359. Tapestries of life

360. Fresh starts
361. Unearthing treasures
362. Harmonious chords
363. Captivating stories
364. Effervescent bubbles
365. Waking up rested

GOOD AT LIST:

1. Communication
2. Time Management
3. Problem Solving
4. Decision Making
5. Emotional Intelligence
6. Integrity
7. Teamwork
8. Leadership
9. Adaptability
10. Conflict Resolution
11. Critical Thinking
12. Empathy
13. Negotiation
14. Networking
15. Financial Management
16. Creativity
17. Resilience
18. Project Management
19. Self-Care
20. Goal Setting
21. Strategic Planning
22. Public Speaking
23. Active Listening
24. Perseverance
25. Self-Discipline
26. Flexibility
27. Motivation
28. Organization
29. Delegation

30. Positive Thinking
31. Building Relationships
32. Work-Life Balance
33. Self-Motivation
34. Writing Skills
35. Technical Proficiency
36. Efficient Reading
37. Innovation
38. Humility
39. Cultural Awareness
40. Digital Literacy
41. Observation
42. Coaching and Mentoring
43. Mediation
44. Assertiveness
45. Collaboration
46. Attention to Detail
47. Customer Service
48. Marketing
49. Salesmanship
50. Negotiation Skills
51. Conflict Management
52. Adaptability
53. Mental Agility
54. Facilitation
55. Mindfulness
56. Gratitude
57. Accountability
58. Analytical Skills
59. Trust-Building

60. Creativity
61. Understanding Body Language
62. Goal Alignment
63. Innovation Management
64. Self-Reflection
65. Emotional Regulation
66. Visual Communication
67. Persuasion
68. Maintaining Boundaries
69. Decision Analysis
70. Information Technology
71. Language Skills
72. Stress Management
73. Generosity
74. Social Responsibility
75. Conflict Negotiation
76. Ethical Judgement
77. Reading Comprehension
78. Storytelling
79. Optimism
80. Delegation
81. Multitasking
82. Data Interpretation
83. Diplomacy
84. Interpersonal Skills
85. Branding
86. Resource Management
87. Strategic Communication
88. Thought Leadership
89. Self-Care Routines

90. Personal Development
91. Gratitude
92. Altruism
93. Friendship
94. Collaboration
95. Trustworthiness
96. Positivity
97. Listening
98. Relationship Management
99. Self-Awareness
100. Curiosity
101. Initiative
102. Mindset Management
103. Educational Knowledge
104. Technical Skills
105. Social Media Management
106. Innovation
107. Presentation Skills
108. Personal Branding
109. Body Language
110. Authenticity
111. Resilient Thinking
112. Feedback Utilization
113. Stress Reduction Techniques
114. Humor
115. Simplicity
116. Public Speaking
117. Budgeting
118. Reliability
119. Impactful Writing

120. Crisis Management
121. Retirement Planning
122. Volunteering
123. Multilingual Abilities
124. Personal Finance
125. Parenting Skills
126. Travel Experience
127. Digital Etiquette
128. Being Punctual
129. Language Learning
130. Compassion
131. Dedication
132. Friendliness
133. Passion for Learning
134. Health Management
135. Courtesy
136. Body Language Reading
137. Foresight
138. Consistency
139. Emotional Literacy
140. Courtesy
141. Mindfulness Meditation
142. Open-Mindedness
143. Self-Improvement
144. Patience
145. Career Planning
146. Spontaneity
147. Gratitude Practice
148. Facilitating Conversations
149. Multicultural Understanding

150. Visionary Thinking
151. Decision Making
152. Empowerment
153. Resourcefulness
154. Goal Visualization
155. Risk Assessment
156. Change Management
157. Positive Reinforcement
158. Influence
159. Reduction of Negative Thinking
160. Volunteer Work
161. Eco-Consciousness
162. Clarification
163. Curating Information
164. Home Management
165. Artistic Skills
166. Rehabilitation
167. Quality Management
168. Balanced Living
169. Joyfulness
170. Health & Wellness
171. Writing
172. Subject Matter Expertise
173. Positive Mindset
174. Self-Expression
175. Self-Initiated Learning
176. Assessing Opportunities
177. Analytical Interpretation
178. Psychological Insight
179. Digital Savviness

180. Problem Identification
181. Family Bonding
182. Attentiveness
183. Gratitude Journaling
184. Presentation
185. Food Preparation
186. Gardening
187. Ethical Living
188. Mind Mapping
189. Social Engagement
190. Meditation
191. Public Relations
192. Protecting Privacy
193. Talent Recognition
194. Constructive Criticism
195. Budget Management
196. Self-Care Practices
197. Business Acumen
198. Ethical Decision-Making
199. Quality Assurance
200. Nutrition
201. Compassionate Leadership
202. Self-Confidence
203. Reading People
204. Thoughtfulness
205. Negotiation
206. Stress Relief
207. First Aid
208. Self-Appreciation
209. Information Analysis

210. Effective Writing
211. Workshop Facilitation
212. Caring for Others
213. Longevity Planning
214. Political Awareness
215. Team Motivation
216. Peacekeeping
217. Teaching
218. Calming Techniques
219. Relationship Building
220. Talent Development
221. Data Management
222. Fitness
223. Mindfulness Retreats
224. Publishing
225. Scripting
226. Validation
227. Work Ethic
228. Cross-Training
229. Obtaining Feedback
230. Fashion Sense
231. Social Skills
232. Content Creation
233. Presentation Layout
234. Disaster Response
235. Digesting Information
236. Reporting
237. Business Planning
238. Time Blocking
239. Webinar Hosting

240. Fair Play
241. Scent Sensitivity
242. Socializing
243. Tech-Savvy
244. Art Appreciation
245. Conversational Skills
246. Active Engagement
247. Charitable Work
248. Online Etiquette
249. Community Service
250. Body-Mind Connection
251. Compliance
252. Donation Practices
253. Facilitating Learning
254. Trust Establishment
255. Productivity
256. Marital Harmony
257. Habits Creation
258. Childcare
259. Open Communication
260. High Energy
261. Social Responsibility
262. Clinical Thinking
263. Volunteerism
264. Event Planning
265. Economic Responsibility
266. Entrepreneurship
267. Managing Expectations
268. Organic Living
269. Forum Engagement

270. Personnel Management
271. Forgiveness
272. Retirement Counseling
273. Reviewing & Editing
274. Sustainability
275. Milestone Tracking
276. Participative Decision Making
277. Family Management
278. Intuition
279. Career Achievement
280. Performing Arts
281. Daily Affirmations
282. Composure
283. Brand Management
284. Horticulture
285. Conflict De-escalation
286. Relationship Alignment
287. Self-Improvement Classes
288. Flexibility Thinking
289. Positive Attitude
290. Reverse Engineering
291. Being Approachable
292. Setting an Example
293. Information Sharing
294. Video Creation
295. Repurposing Content
296. Knowing Technology
297. Relational Intelligence
298. Building Connections
299. Fitness Regimen

300. Lifestyle Planning
301. Creative Needlework
302. wellbeing
303. Life Coaching
304. Memorization
305. Mindfulness Teaching
306. Green Lifestyle
307. Friendly Interactions
308. Task Management
309. Reflective Practice
310. Identifying Weaknesses
311. Business Management
312. Addressing Criticism
313. Adaptation to Growth
314. Gamification
315. Building Influence
316. Time Estimation
317. Career Mobility
318. Tactical Planning
319. Mobile Literacy
320. Meditation Practice
321. Individual Responsibility
322. Project Coordination
323. Parenting
324. Freelancing
325. Persistence
326. Health Awareness
327. Caregiving
328. Generating Solutions
329. Organizational Development

330. Responding to Feedback
331. Family Time
332. Artistic Appreciation
333. Deriving Insights
334. Leveraging Resources
335. Mental Health Maintenance
336. Implementing Plans
337. Calculative Thinking
338. Global Awareness
339. Motivating Others
340. Home Economics
341. Professional Boundaries
342. Financial Planning
343. Tenacity
344. Engagement
345. Ergonomics
346. Architectural Planning
347. Community Involvement
348. Networking & Socializing
349. Trust Building
350. Developmental Psychology
351. Investigative Skills
352. Cultivating Wellness
353. Brainstorming
354. Empathetic Listening
355. Systematic Reviews
356. Social Interaction
357. Professionalism
358. Time Sensitivity
359. Cross-Cultural Awareness

360. Brand Recognition
361. Investigative Research
362. Servant Leadership
363. Clean Living
364. Balanced Eating
365. Personal Fulfillment

GOALS LIST:

1. Brush teeth twice a day.
2. Drink eight glasses of water daily.
3. Read a book each month.
4. Exercise for 30 minutes a day.
5. Meditate daily.
6. Write in a journal every evening.
7. Cook a new recipe weekly.
8. Spend 15 minutes on self-care daily.
9. Save a specific amount of money each month.
10. Organize a room in the house.
11. Call a family member weekly.
12. Volunteer monthly.
13. Walk 10,000 steps a day.
14. Reduce sugar intake.
15. Limit screen time before bed.
16. Learn a new word daily.
17. Practice gratitude each morning.
18. Create a monthly budget.
19. Declutter one space a week.
20. Make a daily to-do list.
21. Spend time outdoors daily.
22. Have a date night each week.
23. Plan a vacation.
24. Take a different route to work.
25. Compliment someone daily.
26. Wake up an hour earlier.
27. Try a new hobby.
28. Clean out the wardrobe.
29. Attend a workshop or seminar.

30. Make a bucket list.
31. Start a blog or vlog.
32. Learn a new language.
33. Master a magic trick.
34. Do yoga every morning.
35. Write a letter to a friend.
36. Grow a plant.
37. Have a technology-free day.
38. No fast food for a month.
39. Savor a favorite dessert.
40. Practice deep breathing exercises.
41. Visit a museum or gallery.
42. Try a new sport.
43. Listen to a podcast weekly.
44. Attend a cultural event.
45. Get a massage.
46. Write a poem or story.
47. Paint or draw something.
48. Explore a new town or city.
49. Host a dinner party.
50. Start a gratitude jar
51. Learn to play a musical instrument.
52. Join a community group or club.
53. Set a daily affirmation.
54. Unplug from social media once a week.
55. Take daily vitamins or supplements.
56. Read a self-improvement book.
57. Conduct a random act of kindness weekly.
58. Plan a family game night.
59. Visit a national park.

60. Cook meals at home for a week.
61. Make a vision board.
62. Create a playlist of favorite songs.
63. Get a full night's sleep consistently.
64. Track daily expenses.
65. Set a bedtime routine.
66. Practice speaking in front of a crowd.
67. Attend a live performance.
68. Document a personal daily photo project.
69. Try a new diet for a month (e.g., vegetarian, keto).
70. Write a thank-you note to someone.
71. Spend a day without complaining.
72. Create an emergency fund.
73. Reconnect with old friends.
74. Build a puzzle.
75. Organize a family reunion.
76. Experience a sunrise or sunset.
77. Limit caffeine intake.
78. Plant a tree.
79. Design a personal homepage or website.
80. Research a historical event or figure.
81. Make a scrapbook.
82. Participate in a charity run or walk.
83. Host a garage sale.
84. Learn basic coding.
85. Plan a surprise for someone special.
86. Practice forgiveness and let go of a grudge.
87. Experience a new culture through food.
88. Watch a documentary.
89. Identify three personal strengths.

90. Start a new tradition.
91. Try intermittent fasting for a period.
92. Have a picnic in a park.
93. Take a mental health day.
94. Organize a movie night at home.
95. Try calligraphy or hand lettering.
96. Revisit old hobbies.
97. Create a family tree.
98. Learn to dance.
99. Donate blood.
100. Maintain a zero inbox.
101. Keep a dream journal.
102. Spend a day at the beach.
103. Experience the stars with a telescope.
104. Master a difficult recipe.
105. Build a new habit tracker.
106. Practice daily affirmations in the mirror.
107. Explore virtual tours of world museums.
108. Pick up a new skill from an online course.
109. Attend a networking event.
110. Organize digital files and photos.
111. Discover new music artists.
112. Write a personal mission statement.
113. Organize a monthly family outing.
114. Practice positive self-talk.
115. Learn about a new culture or religion.
116. Enjoy a night of stargazing.
117. Commit to using reusable bags.
118. Organize personal documents.
119. Visit a local farmers market.

120. Attend a professional development class.
121. Try a new fitness class.
122. Keep a weekly gratitude list.
123. Visit a local library.
124. Start a side hustle.
125. Perform a self-care ritual once a week.
126. Learn to knit or crochet.
127. Commit to a skincare routine.
128. Take part in a community garden.
129. Host a virtual coffee chat.
130. Try a new hairstyle.
131. Create a playlist for different moods.
132. Experience a no-spend week.
133. Learn about investing.
134. Participate in a book club.
135. Make homemade gifts.
136. Start a compost bin.
137. Visit a local zoo or aquarium.
138. Try geocaching.
139. Learn origami.
140. Reduce waste and recycle diligently.
141. Discover a new podcast genre.
142. Improve posture with daily exercises.
143. Visit a local landmark.
144. Enjoy a solo date.
145. Take a creativity class (e.g., painting, pottery).
146. Write a short story.
147. Take a day to explore your own town.
148. Improve flexibility with daily stretching.
149. Revamp your wardrobe with minimalism.

150. Take a scenic drive.
151. Create a daily success habit.
152. Enjoy a spa day at home.
153. Learn a new card game.
154. Host a board game night.
155. Explore meditation techniques.
156. Try a new flavor of ice cream.
157. Write a love note to yourself.
158. Create a family photo album.
159. Develop a personal brand.
160. Paint a room a different color.
161. Participate in a fun run.
162. Experience local theater productions.
163. Go on a digital detox weekend.
164. Grow your own herbs.
165. Explore essential oils.
166. Create a disaster preparedness kit.
167. Write a letter to your future self.
168. Attend a food festival.
169. Practice saying 'no' without guilt.
170. Discover local street art.
171. Prepare a gourmet meal.
172. Enjoy a monthly staycation.
173. Host a neighborhood block party.
174. Dive into DIY crafts.
175. Do daily random acts of kindness.
176. Visit a botanical garden.
177. Plan a surprise for someone.
178. Interview someone about their life story.
179. Discover your ancestry through a DNA test.

180. Experience a new cultural event.
181. Photograph a day in your life.
182. Try progressive muscle relaxation.
183. Make a homemade movie night kit.
184. Learn to code a simple app.
185. Start a meditation practice.
186. Run a 5k.
187. Create a vision for your future.
188. Sort and donate old items.
189. Experience a hot air balloon ride.
190. Visit a historical site.
191. Write a thank-you letter to a mentor.
192. Plant a flower garden.
193. Reconnect with nature through hiking.
194. Incorporate affirmations into daily routine.
195. Sleep under the stars.
196. Experience mindfulness outdoors.
197. Research your family history.
198. Initiate a personal development challenge.
199. Start a hobby blog.
200. Learn about a historical figure.
201. Create handmade decorations for an event.
202. Experience a new cultural cuisine.
203. Build something from wood.
204. Attend a local sports event.
205. Start a monthly newsletter.
206. Practice minimalism in one part of life.
207. Visit an art installation.
208. Slow down and enjoy your food mindfully.
209. Organize a small adventure trip.

210. Develop a public speaking skill.
211. Minimize time spent on non-productive activities.
212. Spend more time in nature.
213. Develop a digital detox routine.
214. Organize a talent show.
215. Have a personal photo shoot.
216. Learn about astronomy.
217. Journal your dreams.
218. Storyboard a short film.
219. Cultivate a gratitude practice.
220. Practice an eco-friendly lifestyle.
221. Take a historical tour.
222. Design a workout plan.
223. Enjoy an afternoon tea party.
224. Have a day of pampering.
225. Start a social media project.
226. Create hand-made cards.
227. Write a personal manifesto.
228. Rearrange furniture for a fresh look.
229. Spend time learning chess.
230. Reduce single-use plastics.
231. Dance daily to your favorite song.
232. Take a short nap daily for energy.
233. Seek out solitude for personal reflection.
234. Cultivate a new friendship.
235. Set a new personal record in a workout.
236. Build a family ritual.
237. Explore the night sky.
238. Set monthly book goals.
239. Video chat with a distant friend.

240. Discover a new vegetarian dish.
241. Make progress on a long-term project.
242. Set monthly personal goals.
243. Enjoy a guilt-free afternoon break.
244. Make a handmade gift for someone.
245. Create a playlist for relaxation.
246. Have a monthly themed dinner night.
247. Set a challenge for the month.
248. Have an eco-friendly month.
249. Take a digital course.
250. Learn a new culinary skill.
251. Plan a themed picnic.
252. Enjoy a full-fledged breakfast buffet at home.
253. Be part of a community service project.
254. Participate in a discussion forum.
255. Develop a sense of work-life balance.
256. Set goals using the SMART method.
257. Maintain a successes and failures diary.
258. Serve at a local soup kitchen.
259. Hold a garage sale.
260. Attend a book signing event.
261. Make a scrapbook of memories.
262. Express creativity through doodling.
263. Cook a family recipe.
264. Engage in a random conversation with a stranger.
265. Celebrate a small achievement.
266. Visit an unfamiliar area of town.
267. Explore a local thrift store.
268. Walk barefoot on the grass or sand.
269. Learn a new dance move.

270. Make someone smile every day.
271. Take part in a career workshop.
272. Create a photo collage.
273. Try out an escape room challenge.
274. Redecorate a room using creative ideas.
275. Share positive stories with others.
276. Develop a simple evening routine.
277. Go to a drive-in movie.
278. Transcribe your favorite song.
279. Make your own pizza from scratch.
280. Do a detox for a day.
281. Obtain a library card.
282. Tell a friend you appreciate them.
283. Draft a family newsletter.
284. Watch a sunrise.
285. Write a letter to your past self.
286. Attend a free community event.
287. Document a time-lapse of your city.
288. Unplug for an entire weekend.
289. Volunteer to read to children.
290. Participate in a car-free day.
291. Take a vow of silence for a specific period.
292. Find a new local café.
293. Be open to new cultures.
294. Discover local legends and folklore.
295. Create a time capsule.
296. Write a blog post about your passions.
297. Visit a flea market.
298. Track mood changes daily.
299. Perform weekly tech cleaning (email/apps).

300. Declutter a neglected space.
301. Learn basic sign language.
302. Have a pet therapy session.
303. Set up a lemonade stand for charity.
304. Listen to a new music genre.
305. Take a pottery or ceramics class.
306. Join a fitness challenge.
307. Start a gratitude chain with friends.
308. Host a themed potluck.
309. Visit a local farm or orchard.
310. Take lessons in photography.
311. Have a zero-emission day.
312. Learn to make homemade candles.
313. Participate in a town hall meeting.
314. Develop a skincare routine.
315. Practice non-dominant hand writing.
316. Visit a lighthouse.
317. Explore a local hiking trail.
318. Learn how to fix a household item.
319. Make handmade bath products.
320. Attend a virtual reality experience.
321. Host a live social media session.
322. Try out a crafting project with friends.
323. Create a personal mission board.
324. Design your own personal logo.
325. Plan a surprise birthday event.
326. Write a children's story.
327. Discover international snacks.
328. Learn a traditional dance.
329. Attend a protest or rally for a cause you believe in.

330. Have a mindfulness walk in nature.
331. Plant a vegetable garden.
332. Visit a country or state fair.
333. Try belly dancing.
334. Learn about a new animal species.
335. Experience candlelit dinners without technology.
336. Write a letter to editors about an issue.
337. Practice empathy by understanding different views.
338. Learn to brew your own coffee or tea.
339. Cultivate a home herb station.
340. Draw or sketch regularly.
341. Write a song or rap.
342. Learn traditional knitting patterns.
343. Plan and execute a scavenger hunt.
344. Host a cultural exchange dinner.
345. Master a new cooking technique.
346. Develop a travel bucket list.
347. Explore a local haunted place.
348. Build a sandcastle with children.
349. Create an emergency savings plan.
350. Simplify daily routines for efficiency.
351. Have a board game tournament.
352. Go without social media for a month.
353. Enjoy slow food cooking.
354. Create art from recycled materials.
355. Interview elderly about their life stories.
356. STEM-related hobby (e.g., robotics).
357. Discover art, dance, or music therapy.
358. Plan weekly publisher dinner lists.
359. Organize a thought leadership group.

360. Enjoy seasonal fruit creations.
361. Engage seriously in global news.
362. Bridge family and personal traditions.
363. Design personal visual life diagrams.
364. Plant a perennial for beauty.
365. Review & celebrate goals accomplished.

ABOUT THE AUTHOR

LINDA LARSON SCHLITZ MS

Drug-addicted, alcoholic, and suicidal at 21, Linda was going to end it all until a 16-year-old girl told her that God had a purpose for her life. Now, 50 years later, Linda has been a licensed counselor for over 35 years and is an international best-selling author, award-winning speaker, and life coach bringing transformation to broken lives.

Linda is the Owner/CEO of Purpose Driven Recovery Academy LLC, Faucet of HOPE Ministries LLC and has Co-Founded several non-profit organizations that help men and women in recovery from mental illness and substance abuse.

Linda is passionate about helping those who are protectors and providers in the world who are faced with traumatic events and ongoing stress.

Linda's expertise in helping agencies and individuals to identify the impact of PTSD and other challenges and address ill-found ways of coping and find solutions to them, has led to her getting commendations from the Governor of Wisconsin, the Secretary of Workforce Development, and various agencies across the nation.

If you are seeking a fun, educational and transformational speaker, or corporate trainer or coach, look no further.

BOOK LINDA
Go to LindaLarsonSchlitz.com

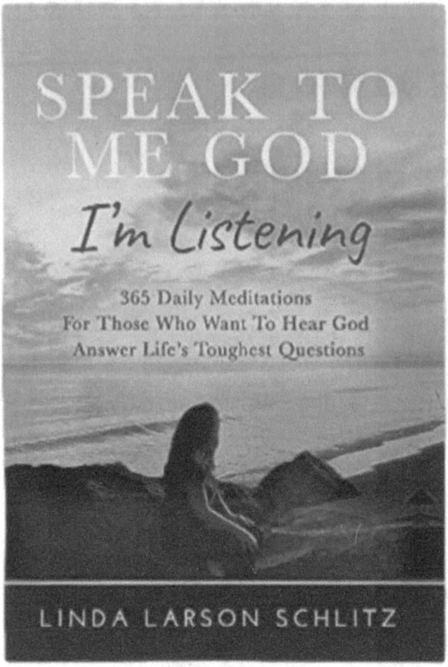

Go to LindaLarsonSchlitz.com to get help today.

If you want to hear God answer your toughest questions, order your Speak to Me God I'm Listening- 365 Daily Meditation Book today on Amazon or in any major bookstore.

ISBN-13 : 978-1640859661

RESOURCES

BOOKS

- Discovering the Brain, Sandra Ackerman Washington (DC): National Academies Press (US); 1992. ISBN-10: 0-309-04529-0
- Who Switched Off My Brain?: Controlling Toxic Thoughts and Emotions by Caroline Leaf | Jan 1, 2009 Switch on Your Brain International, LLC, ISBN-10: 0981956726
- Dopamine Nation: Finding Balance in the Age of Indulgence by Anna Lembke MD, Dutton Publishing 2023 ISBN-10 1524746746
- Speak to Me God, I'm Listening: 365 Daily Meditations for Those Who Want to Hear God Answer Life's Toughest Questions Linda Larson Schlitz, Author Academy Elite Publishing, 2019 ISBN-10: 1640859667
- The Body Keeps The Score: Brain, Mind, and Body in The Healing of Trauma - Paperback by Bessel Van der Kolk M.D. Publisher: Penguin Books Ltd ISBN-10: 0141978619
- High Performance Habits: How Extraordinary People Become That Way, Brendon Burchard, Hay House LLC (Publisher) ISBN-10: 1401964117

PODCASTS

- The Science of Gratitude & How to Build a Gratitude Practice | Huberman Lab Essentials
- Change Your Brain: Neuroscientist Dr. Andrew Huberman | Rich Roll Podcast
- All About Recovery Linda Larson Schlitz: Youtube.com/@LindaLarsonSchlitz

LINKS

- National Child Traumatic Stress Network https://www.nctsn.org/what-is-child-trauma/trauma-types/complex-trauma/effects
- Divorce, Family Arrangements, and Children's Adult Outcomes May 2025
  Written by: ANDREW C. JOHNSTON, MAGGIE R. JONES, AND NOLAN G. POPE
- Working Paper Number: CES-25-28 https://www.census.gov/library/working-papers/2025/adrm/CES-WP-25-28.html
- Green Citizen https://greencitizen.com/blog/can-you-spray-alcohol-on-plants/
- List of 12 Step Links on Wikipedia https://en.wikipedia.org/wiki/List_of_twelve-step_groups
- The Resurgence of the Two-Parent Family Institute of Family Studies Institute for Family Studies https://ifstudies.org/blog/the-resurgence-of-the-two-parent-family
- Psychology of Giving Compliments: The Science Behind Positive Affirmations- Neurolaunch https://neurolaunch.com/psychology-of-giving-compliments/
- Overweight and Obesity Statistics - NIDDK 2017–2018 data from the National Health and Nutrition Examination Survey (NHANES)
- Parental Criticism Worsens ADHD Symptoms - Journal of Abnormal Psychology https://www.apa.org/pubs/journals/releases/abn-abn0000097.pdf
- 86 Billion and Counting - Research on the Brain Alain Goriely Mathematical Institute, Andrew Wiles Building, University of

Oxford, Radcliffe Observatory Quarter, Oxford, OX2 6GG UK https://pmc.ncbi.nlm.nih.gov/articles/PMC11884752/

- Dr. James Dobson- The Role That Parents Play in Self-Esteem https://www.drjamesdobson.org/blogs/sources-of-self-esteem-in-children-part-3-the-role-that-parents-play/

www.ingramcontent.com/pod-product-compliance
Lightning Source LLC
LaVergne TN
LVHW032100210926
848480LV00015B/1454

* 9 7 9 8 9 9 6 4 3 4 4 0 4 *